PARAGON
ISSUES IN
PHILOSOPHY

PARAGON ISSUES IN PHILOSOPHY

African Philosophy: The Essential Readings
Tsenay Serequeberhan, Editor
Critical Theory and Philosophy
David Ingram
Critical Theory: The Essential Readings
David Ingram and Julia Simon-Ingram, Editors
Foundations of Cognitive Science: The Essential Readings
Jay L. Garfield, Editor
Foundations of Philosophy of Science: Recent Developments
James H. Fetzer, Editor
Living the Good Life: An Introduction to Moral Philosophy
Gordon Graham
Living Philosophy
Stephen Rowe
Meaning and Truth: Essential Readings in Modern Semantics
Jay L. Garfield and Murray Kiteley, Editors
Metaphysics: A Contemporary Introduction
John Post
Philosophy and Cognitive Science
James H. Fetzer
Philosophy of Science
James H. Fetzer
Philosophy of Human Rights
Patrick Hayden
Philosophy of Sex and Love: An Introduction
Alan Soble
Philosophy of Sport
Drew Hyland
Philosophy of Technology: An Introduction
Don Ihde
Problems in Personal Identity
James Baillie
Self-Interest and Beyond
David Holley
Social and Political Philosophy
William McBride
Undressing Feminism
Ellen Klein
Woman and the History of Philosophy
Nancy Tuana

THE PARAGON ISSUES IN PHILOSOPHY SERIES

At colleges and universities, interest in the traditional areas of philosophy remains strong. Many new currents flow within them, too, but until recently many of these—the rise of cognitive science, for example, or feminist philosophy—often went largely unnoticed in undergraduate philosophy courses. The Paragon Issues in Philosophy Series responds to both perennial and newly influential concerns by bringing together a team of able philosophers to address the fundamental issues in philosophy today and to outline the state of contemporary discussion about them.

More than twenty volumes are scheduled; they are organized into three major categories. The first covers the standard topics—metaphysics, theory of knowledge, ethics, and political philosophy—stressing innovative developments in those disciplines. The second focuses on more specialized but still vital concerns in the philosophies of science, religion, history, sport, and other areas. The third category explores new work that relates philosophy and fields such as feminist criticism, medicine, economics, technology, and literature.

The level of writing is aimed at undergraduate students who have little previous experience studying philosophy. The books provide brief but accurate introductions that appraise the state of the art in their fields and show how the history of thought about their topics has developed. Each volume is complete in itself but also aims to complement others in the series.

Traumatic change characterized the twentieth century, and the twenty-first will be no different in that regard. All of its pivotal issues will involve philosophical questions. As the editors at Paragon House continue to work with us, we hope that this series will help encourage the understanding needed in a new millennium whose times will be as complicated and problematic as they are promising.

John K. Roth
Claremont McKenna College

Frederick Sontag
Pomona College

LIVING PHILOSOPHY

Remaining Awake and Moving Toward Maturity in Complicated Times

STEPHEN ROWE

LIVING PHILOSOPHY

Remaining Awake and Moving Toward Maturity in Complicated Times

PARAGON ISSUES IN PHILOSOPHY

PARAGON HOUSE ✦ ST. PAUL

First Edition 2002

Published in the United States by
Paragon House
2700 University Avenue West
St. Paul, MN 55114

Library of Congress Cataloging-in-Publication Data

Rowe, Stephen C., 1945-
Living philosophy : remaining awake and moving toward maturity in complicated times / Stephen Rowe. — 1st ed.
p. cm. -- (Paragon issues in philosophy)
Includes bibliographical references and index.
ISBN 1-55778-817-0 (pbk. : alk. paper)
1. Philosophy. 2. Life. I. Title. II. Series.
BD435.R68 2002
100—dc21

2002010031

For current information about all releases from Paragon House, visit the web site at http://www.paragonhouse.com

I am grateful for the support and perspective of students and colleagues in our philosophical community at Grand Valley State University, and especially for the patience and companionship in this project of our Department Coordinator, Cheryl Jones. This book is dedicated to my son, Kevin, whose presence throughout the composing process challenged and inspired.

This book is oriented to leading an "examined life." This means one is engaged in a conscious, relational practice of alertness or full presence, one that cultivates continued growth toward human maturity—or wisdom.

The period of Analytical Philosophy has ended, dialogue with the East has opened, Feminist and Environmental philosophy emerge, and the real and practical value of the original Socratic philosophy becomes accessible again.

CONTENTS

CHAPTER ONE

EXPERIENCING PHILOSOPHY

PHILOSOPHY CAN HELP! It can help us remain awake in times when seductions to falling asleep are many. It can help us grow into the mature humanity our planet requires if life in any way we know it is to survive, if we are to survive.

Philosophy is a human activity that occurs only in the present. It leads to the distinctively human way of being and relating—but one that is largely forgotten in our world of technology, business, and entertainment. "Philosophy," in the sense that most people think of it, as subject matter or academic discipline, is only "left-overs," remains of people having done philosophy in the past.

What is this activity called philosophy? What are its benefits—what can it do for us, and why should we invest any time/energy in its pursuit? How do I know when it is occurring?

In this chapter I begin with a response to these foundational questions, as "close to the ground" as possible, with an attempt simply to describe philosophy when it happens—as an essential life discipline, a hygiene, and an experience that is curiously both more ordinary and more extraordinary than most people think.

But philosophy in the secondary sense, as a subject matter and a history, needs to be taken seriously also. It is not only the record of what others have thought and said, but also the statement of what we, in both broadly historical and more immediately personal senses, have said and learned; it is articulation of our basic commitments, of the causes we are willing to die for—as Socrates was willing to die for truth.

This sense of wonder is the mark of the philosopher. Philosophy indeed has no other origin....[1]

Socrates, *Theaetetus*

...Few professors today could comfortably open their philosophy courses by saying, "If you hope to acquire not just knowledge but wisdom; you must change your lives. You must try to tell the truth. You must cease to live in your skin-encapsulated egos with their petty wishes and try instead to identify yourself with the all-embracing Self. Seek God, pray." If on rare occasion a Western philosopher should now say something like this, it would probably be in a course on ethics or aesthetics, not metaphysics or epistemology. Yet this is the way wisdom philosophers (jnana yogins) used regularly to speak.[2]

Huston Smith

The essential substance of human selfhood lives and grows through the experiences of truth. That is its food. But in the mysteriously and awesomely damaged world of human society, as we know it, truth is not offered in any digestible form to the growing child. Something quite the opposite is offered and, in countless forms, the intimate sense of self is compelled to retreat into a "subconsciousness" that is unknown to modern psychology. It is a subconsciousness that is higher than the ordinary self, not lower; the subconsciousness of finer perception as opposed to the subconsciousness of repressed biological need. This "metaphysical repression" is the great wound shared by every man and woman born into the "world."[3]

Jacob Needleman

I tell you that to let no day pass without discussing goodness and the other subjects about which you hear me talking and examining both myself and others is really the very best thing that a man [*sic*] can do and that life without this sort of examination is not worth living.[4]

Socrates, *Apology*

You and I talk. It has to be real: talk about something that truly concerns us as human beings, about something on which our humanity depends. There must be an atmosphere of compassion or caring, a pervading mutual concern for liberation and growth; not just for winning points in a debate, or impressing each other, manipulating, or maneuvering for the dominant position. It is perhaps a rare thing, this essential human relationship, this way of both individuality and community.

I become aware of the importance of this encounter through its results: the essential relationality makes me more fully who I am at my best, it leads to peace and harmony with others, and goodness occurs when it occurs.

In the faith that articulation can be helpful in our efforts to actually live and benefit from this way of being human, I now move to an attempted description of the internal dynamics of this relationship—so we can begin to make some markings in this crucial territory, some kind of chart or model. What else should "philosophy" be about, than pointing to the nexus of vitality in human life?

In our talking, I struggle to tell you my problem—for example, the problem of my writing, whether I have anything to say that could make any difference, whether anyone reads the sort of book I write anymore, whether screenplay is the only genre that makes sense in our time. In our interaction, what is in question is some aspect of the world, but I am in question also, the worth of my work, and whether I can find a meaningful connection with the world as it is today. Ours is not an abstracted or "academic" conversation.

You listen. You ask for clarification and more full statement; you care enough to ask a hard question; you point out an ambiguity and a contradiction in what I've said, and perhaps a sense in which my ego has gotten in the way of my seeing clearly.

In the face of questioning, I trust you and the context of our encounter enough to get beyond my initial defensive reflexes, beyond ever-lurking duel temptations: either to rationalize a hard or absolutistic legitimation for my position, or to manipulate you by soft though forceful emotionalizing. Either way, I would have have drawn back from relationship, into my defenses and mere competitiveness. If I did this I would not be present any longer, and I would by this act end the relationship in its distinctiveness and significance.

If I can actually consider what is revealed in the midst of our encounter, through your observations and questions, relationship continues. Revelation may take some time to be clear, and even go beyond the moment of our face to face encounter (our relationship, if it is real and strong, continues within me even when we are not together). The considering of what you have revealed occurs in a space within myself that is deeper than my defenses and my wishes to manipulate others (including myself). This space makes it possible for me to transcend myself in the usual sense of "self"—and to grow through our encounter.

This very particular human space—one that can be difficult to get to, even requiring a certain death experience—is sometimes described as Socratic "not knowing" *(aporia),* as in the famous statement that "The wisest of you men [*sic*] is he who has realized, like Socrates, that in respect to wisdom he is really worthless" (sometimes appropriated as "the one thing I know is that I know nothing").[5] This state of not-knowing is not well understood or valued in the culture in which we live—any more than is the state of full presence that issues from it. In fact, most people rush from this state: they change the channel, medicate themselves, diagnose the state of not-knowing as depression or being overly sensitive. It is amazing what people will do to avoid aporia. But an essential part of the Socratic magic, in what Huston Smith and others have observed as the "forgotten truth" at the heart of all the great traditions,[6] is that if I can tolerate this state of not-knowing, I begin to experience possibility, expansiveness, and genuineness. The immediate problem about which we began to converse turns out to be a doorway onto a whole different dimension, a different way of being. I wonder.... I experience wonder. It is as though I *become* wonder.

* * *

Philosophy is occurring.

The wonder is bittersweet. It opens me up to a sort of fresh air; it gets me out of myself. The state of wonder releases me—the real me—from bondage to my own ego, and its ridiculous insistence that it knows and controls everything.

But coming to this crucial state is strenuous and threatening. It makes me vulnerable, or so it seems. For if our encounter is real, it involves the collapse of what I thought I knew, and the discovery that I don't know. This is uncomfortable; sometimes it is downright painful. (It is like the treacherous flight between Shanghai and Tokyo: it is a passage through unstable air that can throw around even 747s, bringing the very fact of existence into question with a distinctly nonintellectual, totally experiential immediacy.)

The state of wonder occurs when I resist the temptation to shut down the conversation and retreat into my defenses, again, through either assertion of a rationalization or an emotionalization. When I am brought to one of those challenging moments that forces me to let go of what I thought I knew and what I thought defended me, the state of not-knowing sets in and is followed by a sort of rebirth. Out of the death of my ego-self my genuine self is born. My ego-self turns out to be a sort of egg....

Philosophy is the pecking from inside and out that lets the little bird of genuine self be born. It is for this reason that Socrates was referred to as a midwife—and also as a flat stingray or torpedo fish![7]

The birth is gaining access to my own wisdom or vitality, to the place in myself through which genuineness flows, though it flows at a slow trickle most of the time, mixed ambiguously with my ignorance, arrogance, and fear. In the moment of rebirth, it is as though the stream flows strong and unobstructed.

Wonder, as the state of access to the energies of genuine self, can also be described as a silence or emptiness (in the Eastern or mystical sense) in that it is experience of the source of knowing, rather than the knowing of this or that in particular. This fundamental human experience is difficult to articulate because it is an experience that cannot be contained in any description that objectifies. It is more an experience of opening, possibility—or freedom, that which is prior to and the origin of any speech or action.

Going back to the Needleman statement at the head of this chapter, the aporia experience of "not-knowing" is paradoxically also experience of truth. It may entail experience of a truth, the truth about one thing or another, but more fundamentally the experience I am trying to describe is also the experience of Truth itself. Truth in this sense is not a product of reason, but an unveiling of reality (as in the Greek *a-lethia,* the lifting of a veil). It is experienced as the expansiveness, openness, and sense of possibility for the good I have tried to describe.[8] It is what Vaclav Havel is talking about when he speaks of "living in truth" rather than in the lies of ideology.[9] It is what Hannah Arendt speaks of when she defines truth as communication, as a kind of relationship, as an event rather than an object.[10]

This is the way of philosophy. It is active—it is about questions, confrontation, and the experience of what William James described as "the death-like termination of certain mental states...."[11] But it must be passive also—receptive. It must be open. True philosophy must forgo control and be willing to accept what happens, what is revealed, what appears. In this regard the practice of philosophy may be helpfully supplemented by the practice of meditation and intimate relationship, both of which are more oriented to the receptive mode—though they, no less than the conversational relationship of philosophy, fail if they do not include the active mode as well. Indeed, philosophy that is not concerned with politics and social change is incomplete at best, and can be dangerous in various ways—for example, in fascist philosophies that are too tight, and in "go with the flow" philosophies that are too loose.

As we do philosophy together, I may find that my problem is surprisingly solved or dissolved, or I may see it in a new light such that it becomes more an opportunity than a problem, or I may wake up the next day with a crucial insight that somehow emerges as a consequence of our interaction. I might also find that my problem is deeper and more frightening than I had thought.

The claim of philosophy—as practice of the Socratic "examined life" (see quote at the beginning of this chapter)—is that if I dare submit to this kind of asking and answering, this way of being with other human beings (including myself), then the mysterious and precious moments of wonder that naturally occur will expand and deepen, gradually transforming the whole of my life from egotism to genuineness.

* * *

Actually, isn't it fairly obvious that life itself is tuned to this same transformative process? Isn't this process familiar to any of us who have experienced the joys and struggles of genuine friendship, or who have merely survived life and its inevitable crises for some time? Again and again we experience the "death" of whatever expectation to which we had become attached, and with which we had identified ourselves. Out of this death we experience the threat of radical uncertainty, and the real possibility of either retreat into defensive bitterness, or stepping out in aggressive assertion—neither of which is faithful to who we really are (a friend would say, in either case, "That's just not you!"). But if we are fortunate, we experience the birth of new life in both ourselves and the relationship. This movement seems fundamental to how human beings grow, progressively learning to know and trust that which is truly trustworthy, and finally resting in a vitality of both reality and self that is beyond ego illusions. Call it God or Tao, Manitou, Knowing Nothing, Truth, or many other names—it is the One source of the many.

Hence we can say that the practice of philosophy is a nurturing along of a process that is quite natural and already occurring.[12]

And note that within this process "philosophy" in a second (and secondary) sense of that term is really unavoidable. Here I speak of philosophy as the humanly necessary codifications of value, articulations of life-direction, and commitments—whether they be mine or someone else's. Philosophy in the second sense is unavoidable because in the process of maturation we need to become conscious of the set of values, meanings, and assumptions that informs our choices and actions. Otherwise we are at the mercy of assumptions that were placed in us in preconscious childhood, running on an "automatic pilot" that does not fly toward fulfillment. The activity of philosophy liberates us (as in liberal education) from assumptions and values, at least some of which we disagree with once we become conscious of them.

In the second sense, philosophy is also the position we take on matters of importance in life, the expectations we harbor, the thoughts we hold, the formulations we employ to resolve the otherwise unbearable ambiguity of existence. Unfortunately, these formulations of position are what remain most accessibly as "the history of philosophy," with the various philosophers of the canon and their intellectual systems. I say "unfortunate" because almost nothing remains of the relationships and the actual lives—the practice of philosophy in the primary sense—out of which these intellectual objects arose. The traditional identification of philosophy as intellectual object, as noun rather than verb, corresponds with what Alfred North Whitehead called "the fallacy of misplaced concreteness."[13] This failing to remember the primary, practical meaning of philosophy has had tragic results in Western history, results William James referred to as products of "vicious intellectualism."[14]

But, again, philosophy in the secondary sense of the problematic "knowing" of the ego is inevitable. And it has its positive side, corresponding with our ability to grow up and overcome unfortunate and even oppressive childhoods as well as with our human ability to make promises and policy, to act consistently on behalf of love and justice. It is politically irresponsible to think that we can live without philosophy in that secondary sense. We must begin our practice of philosophy by humbly stating what our philosophy really is.

There can be terrible consequences if we presume to be "beyond philosophy" prematurely. Philosophy in the first and primary sense of the word, as activity of asking and answering and coming to know nothing, would not be possible without the second sense, any more than a chicken would be possible without an egg! Here is the paradox of philosophy: philosophy in the primary sense seeks to move beyond philosophy in the secondary sense. Honoring the fullness of this paradox, I think it is especially important in our era not to downplay the secondary sense, in the midst of a culture of cynicism, mocking, and "deconstruction" that is not at all the same as the "examination" of philosophy in the primary sense. More on this later, but for now we just need to be aware of the danger of premature or incomplete forms of "knowing nothing."

(Personal note: I prefer to think of philosophy in the primary sense as a necessary and ongoing hygiene. Just as teeth need to be brushed each day, so my ego just naturally generates a kind of knowing—called philosophy in the secondary sense—that will ossify and harden if it is not cleaned out each day by practice of the examined life. This, I take it, is why Socrates tells us we should "let no day pass" without practice of the examined life.)

* * *

This last insight is also fundamental to the tradition of education that arose from the Socratic understanding of philosophy as practice of "the examined life." It is still possible for us today to see that the moving inspiration of liberal education is not just training or information, but something larger, and something intimately connected with the fullness of human growth and development. Any real education is concerned with liberation, with freeing us from the inevitable narrowness of any cultural inheritance—including a culture of cynicism, endless criticism, sensationalism, relativism, skepticism, "whatever" (that narrowness that pretends to be open). Education in the Western vision is concerned not just with information but with transformation. The word itself—in Latin, *educare*—means to lead out or draw forth; to facilitate the birth of the real self from the egg of illusion and egotism in which it is initially contained on this planet.

* * *

This book is a plea for the recovery of philosophy and liberal education as a most effective support for the human development we so urgently need today. But with philosophy there is no such thing as a plea that is separate from practice, from the actual doing of it. For philosophy is one of those basic human activities that can be understood only in its reality from the inside, from the perspective of engagement. So my intention is to do philosophy with the reader as a way of seeking to persuade us to revive and honor this discipline of transformation. If there is any value to this book, it lies in that doing, one that is hard to describe since it is an art, not a science; a practice, not a procedure. Teaching by doing rather than by describing and dictation is always the more effective course, though it is more delicate also.

Below is my plan for the book. In general, it follows the same progression as that of the experience of philosophy described at the beginning of this chapter.

CHAPTER 1

First, we must make contact with our own direct experience of the transformation process I've just briefly described. No further talk of philosophy is of any real value until there is contact with the process itself from within the textures of our own actual experience. I am hoping your dialogue with what has already been said in this chapter has facilitated this contact; I am hoping you are in touch with those questions and conversations in your life that are doorways to wonder and truth. In the words of Rilke's famous *Letters to a Young Poet,* I am hoping you know how to "...love the questions themselves.... Live the questions now."[15]

CHAPTER 2

Second, especially because of the prejudices and stereotypes about "philosophy" (mostly justified) that float around our cultural environment, we need some discussion of method and actual practice of philosophy. I hope the discussion of Chapter 2 can prepare the reader at several levels for what follows in the rest of this book, especially in terms of the immediate practice of reading a book. This preparation is necessary because, in addition to the prejudices I mention, we have a tendency to admire cultural resources from afar rather than actually engaging them. My emphatic point is that philosophy is only worthwhile—and even visible—if we actually practice it! In order to make the practice more vivid and accessible, Chapter 2 contains a Core Bibliography and an X-ray View of the dialogue of this book. This chapter aims to establish philosophy as relational, communal, and active in relation to both self and society.

CHAPTER 3

Third, in order to move to a more effective practice of philosophy, we need perspective on the function of human knowing, and "philosophy" in the second sense of the term—as interpretations we create, accept, or simply internalize, and that we share with others in varying degrees of compassionate persuasiveness, defensiveness, or aggression. To practice philosophy well, we must learn to take our interpretations seriously: we need to face them, evaluate them, take responsibility for them, and refine them. We need to enter a process in which we move gradually toward "not knowing" through a series of knowings or interpretations.

CHAPTER 4

In Chapter 4 I seek to identify and evaluate the predominant interpretations of our day in both theory and practice. The first two main philosophies I call "Easy-Life-ism" and "Machine-ism." The third philosophy is "The Psychological Worldview," which also serves as the main framework within which problems of other philosophies are treated today. Chapter 4 winds up being very critical of the dominant psychological worldview of our era, but the next chapter offers an alternative that is present in our era also—including perspective on the development we must all endure and learn to enjoy as we pass through that phase of development in which the psychological is figural.

CHAPTER 5

In Chapter 5, then, I try to articulate a more humanly adequate philosophical orientation that is arising in our midst, called "The Philosophy of Human Development." This other possibility is oriented to a vision of human maturity, one that is compatible with the traditional Socratic practice. I have already given some pretty substantial hints as to this developmental vision, culminating in the kind of human being who can both "know nothing" and be responsible in their choice of interpretations.

CHAPTER 6

In this somewhat experimental chapter I share some insights and sources that have been helpful in my own practice, and also present a model as to what might constitute an effective philosophical journal as an aid to individual growth. Here I have no choice but to write very close to the ground of my own actual experience of attempting to live a human life in these times.

CHAPTER 7

The concluding chapter speaks primarily from the service dimension of philosophy, about a vision and political direction in relation to what the world might become. This chapter raises the issue of human development on the historical scale, representing the voice of the philosophical orientation I advocate, now spoken in the larger world of intercultural dialogue and "new world order."

And about this book *overall,* I want to say what I hope is already obvious: that the plan for this book must be conversational rather than treatise-oriented, oriented to relational practice rather than simply to the construction and delivery of intellectual objects. The structure of the book itself reflects the fact that there are, in the words of Elizabeth Kamarck Minnich, "several different ways to move into the conceptional center," and therefore the possibility of a structure of "...circlings in and out: we are exploring a whole here, not tracing a line or making an argument or proving a point."[16] Yet this structure will not be effective without the conversational engagement of the reader.

* * *

In "The Phaedo," the dialogue that concludes with Socrates' execution, Socrates speaks of there being "a frightened child" within each one of us, and of the need to "sing charms and incantations" in order to calm this child. He likens philosophy to this singing—and he also defines philosophy as preparation for death and dying.

In the same dialogue Socrates pulls back from speculation about life after death and other metaphysical matters. At one point he gives an elaborate depiction of what is above the Earth and below, but then he immediately steps away from the depiction, saying that no sensible person would insist that things are exactly as he has described them. However, he goes on to say that we should "risk the belief" in such things as the immortality of our souls, and repeat it to ourselves "as if it were an incantation...." This is to say that philosophy, as the articulation of what we believe about the nature of reality, our interpretations of things, should be understood pragmatically, as relative to the life we live; there is something of our lives larger and far more important than what we believe, something that our believing either does or does not support. This larger entity Socrates calls "soul," and he defines philosophy as purification and liberation of the soul, and preparation for death.[17]

And note that the interpretation of Socrates I recommend is not the only one that is possible! In the history of Western culture we can see that many schools of philosophy have claimed Socrates as their hero, running the full spectrum from the rationalists/empiricists/analytics on the one end, to the idealist/romanticist/mystical on the other.[18] For example, notice that the analytical philosophers with whom I am in tension can also claim Socrates as their origin and inspiration; it is not difficult to see Socrates as the consummate practitioner of logic and rational argument. There is a sense, then, in which the Greek Socrates is similar to Jesus on the Hebrew side of Western culture: his inspiration is wide, functioning more like an energizing source than a doctrine or final interpretation (though, of course, many have claimed just this—to be in possession of absolute definition). From this broad perspective on the Western drama, we can see that one of the major strands out of which the culture is woven is the conversation about who Socrates really is.[19]

From my own standpoint within the pluralism of Western history, I want to say that not only is Socrates about dialogue, he is dialogue.

* * *

People have learned to think poorly of philosophy. And rightly so. Too frequently "philosophy" has been mere intellectualizing, a retreat from real life into an artificial world of abstraction. Living, breathing, relational life has been violated in the name of merely conceptual order and certainty. Real thought too, as the reflective dimension in the service of a life well lived, has been eclipsed by the rush to "objectivity" and the unexamined practice of intellectualizing.

No wonder so many of us have learned to hate "eggheads" and "ivory tower intellectuals." They are out of touch with what is actually going on, and arrogant to boot! They insult our most noble pragmatic efforts, our real joys and sorrows as human beings.

But wait! Let's not get carried away with the sport of philosopher bashing! In fact, let's shift the perspective just a bit. Don't people love to hate philosophers just a little too much sometimes? And doesn't what and how people hate reveal something very significant about them? Without moving into psychoanalysis, some forms of which bear striking resemblance to the parent discipline of philosophy, I want to suggest that many people like to criticize philosophers so harshly and so automatically because they themselves are intellectualist; the "philosopher" is simply a reflection of us! By this I mean that many, many people, especially in Western societies, live in their heads, only vaguely aware of anything that does not correspond with their more or less rational conclusions drawn from past experience. The point is that they live in and out of unexamined conclusions and the clouds of smoke they maintain around them, some that turn out to be quite bizarre when they are examined in the clear light of day.

Many have observed that our whole culture has become terribly imbalanced in the direction of the intellect, the left brain, the male orientation to abstract rights and rules, etc. And many of the most vital cultural currents of our time seek to correct the imbalance by putting us in touch with the "other" aspect of our humanity which had been suppressed (repressed—and oppressed) for most of the short period of recorded human history: the emotional, the right brain, the feminine, the prehistoric, the Eastern. Think of the underlying claims of the Eastern and mystical influences that are so available today, or relational feminism, or the various schemes to lead us in the direction of holistic living.

My point is that real philosophy has this same aim of restoring human balance and harmony! Philosophy cannot be only the sharpening of critical skills, any more than it can be only the grasping of the history of philosophy. It can be effective for this sharpening, which itself needs an adequate purpose in order to guide it, but philosophy has a much larger aim and intention in relation to the whole of a human life—and one that is inevitably misplaced or violated if we take up philosophy in any of its lesser senses.

The larger aim of philosophy arises from the fact that human beings need direction in life. Unlike other forms of life as we know them, humans cannot live gracefully only through genetic and social conditioning. We need teachers, such that the question of my freedom is not the question of whether or not I will have a teacher, but whether I am capable of becoming my own teacher—and of finding true teachers along the way. And "philosophy" begins to become relevant once I discover that simply following my "feelings" does not lead me in the direction of a life that is loving and just, but rather into incoherence and narcissism. If I am to be my own teacher and healthy in my identification of teachers I must direct myself according to some considered values and commitments, some overall purpose, structure of interpretation, and meaning. Philosophy, as practice of the examined life, helps me become aware of and move in relation to these crucial things, to refine them, and to act effectively on behalf of their embodiment.

Yet the larger aim of philosophy even goes beyond the choosing of a direction in life. It has to do with choosing and rechoosing after the previous choice has proven insufficient, and then finally realizing that my best direction in life involves acceptance of this process itself, and learning to trust a sort of directionless direction—or a sense of both self and direction that can never be objectified, but which is nevertheless the part of me which is most real. Here, again, we come to the mysterious "knowing nothing" of Socrates, that experience of source and living in truth.

* * *

Zen practitioners speak of the need for us to become like clear glass, free of distortion and taint. Some feminists speak of relationship as the space in which the best energies of both ourselves and God become manifest and creatively active in an unfinished world. After the long period of Western intellectualism, do not these voices speak in harmony with Socrates, helping us along the path of development that leads to genuineness?

CHAPTER TWO

THE PRIORITY OF PRACTICE

(Something Like a Syllabus)

OK, PHILOSOPHY—as a way of being, an activity. One envisions someone like Michael Kane in the old *Kung Fu* TV show, living an extraordinary life in the midst of frontier crudeness. But to actually allow any of the great ways of transformation to come into my life, to live it rather than just be entertained by it, takes more than envisioning.

Magnificent human beings do not just happen; the mature human form does not simply unfold out of the natural process, as seems to be the case with other life forms. Mature human beings—even just interesting ones—take work. Behind every significant human life there is some substantial discipline and practice.

The practice is always humbling—and frustrating, "impossible" in relation to the grandeur of the goal anticipated. And it requires the essential glue of authority or grace that keeps the practitioner practicing through those inevitable moments when ego seizes the mind and tells us we can stop the practice. As Aristotle pointed out long ago, it takes persistence along with good reasons and conscious awareness.

...You seem to have this childish fear that the wind would really dissolve and scatter the soul, as it leaves the body, especially if one happens to die in a high wind and not in calm weather.

Cebes laughed and said: "Assuming that we were afraid, Socrates, try to change our minds, or rather do not assume that we are afraid, but perhaps there is a child in us who has these fears; try to persuade him not to fear death like a bogey."

You should, said Socrates, sing a charm over him [*sic*] every day until you have charmed away his fears.[20]

Socrates, *Phaedo*

The ethical self is an active relation between my actual self and a vision of my ideal self as one-caring and cared-for. It is born of the fundamental recognition of relatedness; that which connects me naturally to the other, reconnects me through the other to myself. As I care for others and am cared for by them, I become able to care for myself.[21]

Nel Noddings

This chapter is not fun. It is about the work of philosophy, and it is put together in a systematic way. It is the least "nonlinear" or conversational of the chapters in this book, the most formal. It is about method.

The idea of philosophy as a way of life may sound good, look good, be attractive. However, there is a world of difference between envisioning this ideal (—a crucial first step that many never take), and getting it connected to what we actually do. The question is simple, though not easy: are we willing to engage the humble work of growth and transformation—or not? Without hearing some kind of "Yes," however tentative and ambivalent it may be, it makes no sense to go on. In the absence of this simple but crucial affirmation, philosophy remains a displaced ideal to be admired—or scorned. It can be scorned forcefully, sometimes to "cover" its denial of our humanity (analogous to the scorning of Socrates unto death by the people of Athens).

* * *

Socrates says "...discussing goodness and the other subjects about which you hear me talking and examining both myself and others is really the very best thing a person can do." This claim is much larger than those usually associated with philosophy. What does Socrates mean?

I propose three responses to Socrates through the presentation of this book:

First, this book itself is a practice—or a fruit of someone's practice (mine and my community's). In this regard I offer it for what it may be worth, as an example of an earnest attempt to practice philosophy.

Second, this book is a practice about practice: a practice in which practice itself—as one of those "other subjects," like goodness, in the Socrates statement—is under inquiry. Hence I offer this book as a resource.

Finally, the book you are holding is also an argument for the effectiveness of philosophy—an argument as to why and how we would do well to try philosophy. I mean to recommend that the reader actually consider a certain very old Western practical option from among the smorgasbord of options offered in our cultural moment. For I think that in the midst of the confusions of our culture (when, for example, many Westerners will gladly convert to anything not-Western, or be so overwhelmed that they just watch the TV), philosophy becomes available to us more purely than it has been available for centuries—alongside the riches of the other great traditions of human transformation.

I hope this book will encourage you to make contact with Socrates and experience philosophy as a way of being rather than merely a way of thinking, yet also to experience the relevance of ways of thinking in relation to the most general factor mentioned by Socrates: a life worth living.

* * *

Philosophy is practice of Socrates' "examined life."

Philosophy is a path of transformation and a way of relating to other human beings (and oneself, as Nel Noddings notes in the quote in the beginning of this chapter). The abstractions and systems of thought that are so often identified with philosophy are secondary to the primary practice—as life is prior to thought, and actual is prior to ideal.

As an attempt to pursue this ideal, the Western tradition of liberal education arose. With this Socratic vision, reading and writing were added to conversational encounter as subpractices. Reading is the art of *listening*, and writing the art of *speaking*, and each done properly contributes directly to the larger, inclusive practice of *conversation*. Any educator worth her salt will tell you that we cannot read effectively without speaking or writing in response; and we cannot write effectively without listening to and representing fairly the positions taken by others.

Any teacher who is serious knows how hard it is to hold "reading" and "writing" together. In fact, styles of education in the West can be understood in terms of inability to hold these elements together: some styles overemphasize reading/listening and spawn rebellion against authority in the name of individual freedom, while other styles overemphasize writing/speaking and tend toward the chaos of unbridled individualism. William James had in mind the holding together of these elements and styles when he gave his famous maxim on education: "no impression without correlative expression."[22]

The priority of practice, along with the fact that philosophy moves in the medium of conversation and words, means that it is always appropriate to ask the pragmatic question: "So what? What difference do or would these words, this understanding, or this way of thinking make?" It is important to stay focused on the practical because in our time a very long era of abstraction from life and emphasis on the intellectual is ending, such that the most general challenge before the human race now is one of return, presence, the challenge of living an embodied life on planet Earth. The challenge is to counterbalance and transform the forces of "leaving" (technology, management, capitalism...).[23] It is also important to stay focused because there is so much reaction in our era, assertion of the irrational, mere feelings, self-interest, or, as I have said, premature or misplaced claims to "know nothing." Clarity about the essential elements of healthy practice helps us to stay away from these problems.

I know that what I have just said needs elaboration and is part of a much longer story, but for now I just want to emphasize the importance of remaining conscious about practice and actual results in the world.

* * *

But now back to the immediacy of practice—getting to the particulars:

For me, the most immediate practice right now is writing. For you, the figural practice is reading. I hope you have by now encountered conversation as practice, hopefully one that is now occurring between us, and within each one of us.

In this chapter I need to say a few things about these crucial subpractices of philosophy: reading, writing, and conversation—related to the question as to how this book can be a resource for philosophical practice, and how cultivation of these subpractices in a disciplined sense can contribute to the broader scope of one's whole life. So with discussion of each of the subpractices, I will speak first in broadly cultural terms, and then move to concrete suggestions.

READING

No one reads any more. No one has time—or space, except perhaps for diversionary reading or informational reading. When I say no one reads, I mean reading for a life, in relation to a life—something of the person that is deeper than either the psyche or the intellect, as well as the usual forms of recreation. Maybe this itself has become a foreign or old-fashioned notion: a life and its real needs by way of nurture and discipline.

We watch TV and movies. The chairs in the "living room" no longer face each other before hearth and fire, but that electronic tube connected by cables and airwaves to the global village. In more affluent homes the living room becomes a relic reserved for special occasions while the living goes on in the "family room," and there we invariably find the tube.

I want to turn it off for a few minutes and reflect on the act of reading. I want to speak very concretely about reading as a transformative practice, one that is closely associated with the greatness of the Western tradition.

The first thing to be said is that reading takes—and creates—a very particular sort of time and space. There is a sense in which the very act of reading, the creating and protecting of this space and the coming to it in the midst of a life, is everything. As is the case with other disciplines of transformation, part of the magic of reading lies in what one must do with the rest of one's life in order to make this activity possible.

It is best to find a comfortable place, but not too comfortable;

a posture more erect than that of the TV mode is necessary. And this activity requires certain ancillary equipment: two or three different colored pens with which to mark up the text with underlines and notes in the margin, a pad of paper near the book for further notes, and—perhaps at greater remove from the primary activity of reading—a journal for occasional entries on what you take from the reading and how you respond to what it says.

In relation to the last item, it is important to point out that reading, in the fullness of this practice, entails writing; it is a cooperative and relational practice. We need to come to terms with the definiteness of what the author says, and bring our response to the questions under discussion out of our unconsciousness subjectively, to similar definiteness. At the same time, there is a sense in which a good book will soak up and deliver us from the unproductive and unhappy forms of subjectivity that inhibit our full presence. We need writing in order to achieve the maximum definiteness that is possible through reading.

But none of this will happen without an effective method. Here is what I suggest: read each chapter quickly a first time, with minimal stops for underlining, coffee, or attention to the ever-insistent tasks of routine life. And read actively, which is to say that with each chapter one needs to ask, upon reading the last word, what's the point, and how do I respond? (Both sides of the active dialogue are necessary, both what the book says and what I say in response). Then go back, more slowly, and reread with a different colored pen, marking more passages, getting an accurate understanding of the author's words in dialogue with the depth of your own response. Again, in real reading one reads oneself in dialogue with reading of the text; part of the claim of the reading practice is that it is far more effective than introspection as a way to "know thyself."

Then one must take notes, more formally than on the pad one keeps alongside the text. After underlining and marking the text, it is necessary to get the structure or "x-ray" of the reading down on a page or two of outline notes—out there where you can see it and make it your own. Here I recommend paper with a wide left margin, and a strict separation at this stage between just what the author is saying and how I respond. Finally, one must respond, in that journal or notebook further removed from the text, in full statement—not just notes—to both the book and as the self who is doing the reading. In order to read one must write. These two activities are interdependent, along with an inclusive third activity, that of conversation (that, with one's self, is a vibrant inner life, and with others is the fully human relationship).

This, in brief, is the practice. Of course, we do not engage the full reading practice with all materials that pass before us. It is essential to choose what to read at the first level of quick review and what few substantial texts we will read deeply and fully. Survival, in our era of information explosion, requires choice. Most things I "read" I take up only at the very first level indicated above: I decide not to go further. But the point is that in order to have the benefit of the reading practice I must choose some material through which to enter into the full practice.

At the risk of offending the sophisticated reader, I offer this statement of practice because in my relationships with a broad range of students, citizens, and seekers I am confronted again and again with the same situation: with people who want to read and who have some intuition and partial experience of the significance of this practice, but who do not know how. Usually these same people are confused by the "instant gratification" aspect of TV, actually injured by its superficiality and subliminal message of passivity. Some of my most satisfying moments in teaching consist simply in showing people how to read.

But what of the claim about the significance of reading, its transformative result? What could it mean to speak of reading for a life, that aspect of ourselves that is deeper than diversion, psychological adaptation, or being informed?

Reading is relational. It is a slow-motion and disciplined form of that very encounter we have with people who are physically present to us. Here is the fundamental claim of reading as a discipline, a yoga, a path of transformation: it develops our power to relate, which includes relationship to self as well as other. While reading in general is a practice of relationship, through the selection of our reading we choose those relationships that will literally form us, and thereby also the larger world we create through our vocation, private life, and citizenship. This underlines the importance of selection, sound advice, and choice as to those materials we read fully, an importance that is quite analogous to our selection of food and forms of exercise for physical well-being. Reading for a life nourishes the soul.

Reading elevates our ability to choose and act, and hence our own real presence, our definiteness. For in the act of reading we construct a world in microcosm, a world quite different from that of entertainment. Unlike TV and movies in which so much is "done for us" (and hence to us, through the underlying message of passivity), in reading we become producer and director, casting artist and set designer. And we inevitably become the protagonist as well; the options are ours, the same options that have already been exercised by creators of movies and TV shows—for which there is almost always a script to which viewers do not have access ("In the beginning was the word"—even at the movies). Though the images of TV and movies may be dramatic on the surface, the act of reading brings us into relationship at a deeper level, and in a way that wakes up our real self—the self of a life as opposed to the self of mere functioning. And reading both activates and relaxes, perhaps like good exercise, in contrast to entertainments and substances that provide the illusion of relaxation but actually lead to restlessness.

Today there is great concern in academic circles with "hermeneutics," the act of interpretation that occurs in reading and in all relationships. When this coming to consciousness of the power and complexity of reading does not frighten academics, causing them to "retreat into theory," hermeneutics is a conversation about the deep formation of both person and culture. Reading, like life itself, is relational in that we "produce" texts (and persons) in our act of reading them, an act itself that is always determined in part by our own context of time and place and development, which itself may be changed by the text. This circle, in which we continuously choose both who we will be and what we read (and relate to generally), offers the possibility of real growth—and hence a better world.

But in some ways the recent discovery of these dynamics, despite big claims about "postmodernism" that are frequently associated with it, is really a *re*discovery: of the power of reading which has been honored and valued as a transformative practice in traditional Western culture for many centuries, up to the time in our century of homelessness and suspense when "print culture" was displaced by "electronic culture" and the consumption of everything, including experience.

This rediscovering the West was brought home to me recently when I read an article by a colleague. He tells a very poignant story of the struggle and pain of an Anglo person to find that connection with history and tradition that he, like so many of us today, has found necessary in order to have access to his own vitality. After experimenting with traditions that are "other" to him, he discovered Anglo shamanism. But it turned out that this tradition is available almost exclusively through the reading of texts. My colleague reports this fact almost apologetically: while other appropriations of tradition involve dancing, drumming, and chanting, his becomes available through reading. He goes on to suggest that reading involves "subtle, imaginal experience" and thus is at least as "experiential" as workshops in Connecticut or California. My response was one of being not greatly moved by the possibilities of shamanism as it was described by my colleague, but of being struck very deeply by the image of my colleague in the act of reading, by the nobility of this pursuit.

Toward the end of his article my colleague referred to a story I had heard before about Joseph Campbell, the great collector and celebrator of myths from all over the world. When asked one day if he meditated, Campbell is said to have replied something to the effect that each time he was about to enter this practice it occurred to him that he could be reading instead, and that he chose the latter activity. Up until the day I read my colleague's article I had found this Campbell story troubling, and revealing of what I find very problematic about his "religion"—an interim religion at best, one of admiring "many paths" while walking on none. After I read my colleague's piece I saw Campbell in a different light, still as interim but with a powerful subtext, one that needs to be lifted up and made explicit. I saw the dignity of Campbell as a traditional person and wondered if he was aware of himself in these terms. Could it be that his subtext was reading itself, a traditional Western practice that Campbell, like many of us, overlooked in his enthusiasm for the vivid variety of transformative practices that becomes available from other traditions in our day? This question led me to recall one of my favorite Japanese sayings: "A dunce once went searching for fire with a lighted lantern. Had he known what fire was, he would have eaten his rice much sooner."

WRITING

Writing has already been discussed to some extent under "Reading." They are interdependent arts, especially so as they are embraced by the third subpractice of conversation. The Socratic art of philosophy is above all relational.

With writing as the particular subpractice we want to look at now, we learn "articulation." But this needs to be clearly distinguished from "self-expression," "assertiveness," and advertising. Something much greater than self-interest is occurring in genuine articulation.

Real articulation does indeed involve definite identification of one's own location in relation to whatever problems/issues/questions drive "the writing assignment" (it is impossible to write/articulate in the middle of nowhere—as we discover in the muteness of loneliness, as distinct from the harmony of solitude).

Writing/articulation is not only responsive to problems/issues/questions in the world, but it also involves accurate and sympathetic understanding of the locations and positions of others. Articulation and writing are, again, relational: they require dialogue partners who are different from "self," such that the content of writing/articulation is qualitatively different from the mere revelation of internal psychological content that is so prevalent today. Through writing/articulation, a great and paradoxical truth is discovered: dialogue with the other, not simple emptying of the psyche (which is necessary sometimes, not a bad thing in itself), is the key to letting the true Self emerge.

So far I have spoken about "Writing" in the broader sense, as an art that is fundamental to culture. But we must not neglect the more specific sense of writing, and the ways that the very concrete discipline of philosophy (or liberal education) can help us actually develop the art of articulation/writing in ourselves and others—the practice through which we can have access to "Writing" in the broader terms discussed above.

So, speaking concretely to writing in philosophy, I suggest the following steps, with understanding that in an art any definition of "steps" is partially artificial and variable in their implementation:

1. Awareness of and some initial thinking about the problem/question/issue that is under inquiry. Again, good philosophy never occurs in the middle of nowhere, but with some significant connection to the world. It is also essential in philosophy and the humanities generally, that the problems/questions/issues that launch an inquiry are always matters about which any functioning adult already has some position—whether conscious or not, and about which we are all qualified to think. So job one in writing is to get a good grasp of both that which initiates inquiry, and one's own preliminary thinking in the matter.

2. Resources: apply the reading method discussed above to the readings or resources offered for the particular unit or instance of inquiry. In a course, these are provided and utterly obvious on the class syllabus. In life outside the discipline of a course, appropriate resources, including readings and other people whose thinking on the problem/issue/question need to be attended to and understood. Again, we are rarely alone.

3. Dialogue: working back and forth between steps one and two; letting my own thinking develop in agreement and disagreement with that of the sources, and addressing the sources from the practical standpoint of how they inform my own thinking. This "step," ideally, is present in steps one and two: my thinking is with others, and my appropriation of resources is guided by both the obligation to listen and my own practical concerns.

After these three steps, and the notetaking that go with them, I am ready to enter the zone of writing in the very concrete sense of pencil to paper. Here also I suggest "steps," and again emphasize the necessity of developing a good method.

1. "Sketch": There needs to be a first stage that is very open and playful. Use big newsprint sheets, or an artist's pad, or 3x5 cards and note sheets on a dining room table or big bed.

2. Outline: Construct some kind of x-ray or map of the statement you intend to write. I use these physical terms to distinguish the kind of "outline" I recommend from the formal sort of thing many of us were taught in high school (or somewhere!), a rigid structure of roman numerals, capital letters, small letters and numbers, etc. A useful outline is best thought of as a point of departure, something solid enough to be a launching pad for the act of writing.

3. Draft: It is crucial to do a draft as a letting go and seeing what you say, not a mere "writing up" of a formal outline—as though simply being a secretary to oneself, or just adding the vital fluid to an inflatable body. Writing itself, when it goes well, is an essential part of the process of discovery; when it goes well I always discover myself saying and "knowing" things that are surprising to me. But this cannot happen if the act of writing is too constrained by preconceived—or ill conceived—notions.

4. Edit: At this step we need to apply the same good method of reading that we use with sources to our own work. There are crucial questions that must be addressed: What is the central point of the piece?; what is its structure—the relationship of its parts to the whole?; does it have the right beginning and ending, and the right title?; and what particular parts of the text are either repetitive or not yet fully developed, understandable, or clear?

5. Final: In the end, it requires a decisive act to move from editing to either a fresh draft or submission copy. Here it is important to realize and accept the fact that no writing is perfect or even "complete" until it is delivered to the world—whether in the shape of your professor or some other agency that is willing to take the writing from—and in ways out of—your hands.

CONVERSATION

I've already said much about conversation or dialogue. Perhaps it is sufficient at this point to move very concretely to conversation as it relates to what you are doing right now.

Most books have their bibliography in the back. This book must have the Core Bibliography right up front. The reason is that, as a practice of philosophy (and an argument about philosophy as a practice, and resources for the same), this book emerges out of the Socratic "discussing," out of dialogue or conversation. This book is conversation, slowed down and deliberate enough that it precipitates out as words on paper. It is not treatise; it is not presentation of a settled intellectual formulation, but a doing, an undertaking.

The fact of conversation implies a finite number of dialogue partners. I want to introduce the partners who participate in this book right away, and make them as accessible as possible to the reader. For I am writing, in part, to suggest that conversation with these particular people can be extremely useful in the living of life.

Here, then, is the

CORE BIBLIOGRAPHY

Plato, "The Apology." The classic work in which Socrates speaks of his career overall, of what he is doing and why.[24]

Huston Smith, "Western Philosophy as a Great Religion," in Bryant, ed., *Essays on World Religion.* An inspiring piece that makes available in the present the original, transformative practice of philosophy, along with historical perspective on how it became lost in Western history.[25]

Plato, "The Phaedo." Here Socrates speaks from his last days, about the human condition and its redemption through "recollection," dialogue, and establishing a good relationship with "the frightened child within."[26]

Nel Noddings, "Construction of the Ideal," from *Caring: A Feminine Approach to Ethics and Moral Education.* A presentation of "caring" or relationality as the ideal human state, and discussion of how we can live in the tension between ideals and actualities.[27]

William James, "The Types of Philosophic Thinking," from *A Pluralistic Universe.* A brilliant typology of philosophical approaches and temperments, oriented in terms of the capacity of a philosophy to help us be more at home in our lives and faithful to the world as "our common mother."[28]

Martin Luther King Jr., "The World House," from *Where Do We Go from Here?* A "new classic" that addresses the numbed condition of society today and the "revolution of values" through which it can be overcome.[29]

Masao Abe, "Zen Is Not a Philosophy, But...," from *Zen and Western Thought.* On what Eastern and Western cultures have to contribute to each other, and how they can meet in mutual growth.[30]

Karl Jaspers, "The Maintenance of Selfhood," from *Man in the Modern Age.* Beginning with the idea that philosophy is "the thought with which I am able to be present as my own real self," a description of the "new nobility" that is emerging in the midst of our historical period of transition.[31]

To even further expose and illuminate the conversation of this book, as concretely as possible, I would like to share a few pages of quotes from the same authors mentioned above.

The quotes that follow become a sort of "x-ray": they lift up and reveal the inner structures—the bones—of the book you are reading. They also serve as a preview as well as a menu of authors you may want to consult as you read *Living Philosophy.* It would be my ideal for us to read all of the essays from which quotes are selected, right along with the reading of *Living Philosophy,* in the order indicated above.

AN X-RAY VIEW OF **LIVING PHILOSOPHY**

by Stephen Rowe

Chapter One
DOING PHILOSOPHY

Wonder is the feeling of a philosopher, and philosophy begins in wonder.

Socrates, *Theaetetus*

I tell you that to let no day pass without discussing goodness and the other subjects about which you hear me talking and examining both myself and others is really the very best thing that a man [*sic*] can do and that life without this sort of examination is not worth living.

Socrates, *Apology*

...Few professors today could comfortably open their philosophy courses by saying, "If you hope to acquire not just knowledge but wisdom; you must change your lives. You must try to tell the truth. You must cease to live in your skin-encapsulated egos with their petty wishes and try instead to identify yourself with the all-embracing Self. Seek God, pray." If on rare occasion a Western philosopher should now say something like this, it would probably be in a course on ethics or aesthetics, not metaphysics or epistemology. Yet this is the way wisdom philosophers (jnana yogins) used regularly to speak.

Huston Smith

The essential substance of human selfhood lives and grows through the experiences of truth. That is its food. But in the mysteriously and awesomely damaged world of human society, as we know it, truth is not offered in any digestible form to the growing child. Something quite the opposite is offered and, in countless forms, the intimate sense of self is compelled to retreat into a "subconsciousness" that is unknown to modern psychology. It is a subconsciousness that is higher than the ordinary self, not lower; the subconsciousness of finer perception as opposed to the subconsciousness of repressed biological need. This "metaphysical repression" is the great wound shared by every man and woman born into the "world."

Jacob Needleman

Chapter Two
THE PRIORITY OF PRACTICE
(Something Like a Syllabus)

...You seem to have this childish fear that the wind would really dissolve and scatter the soul, as it leaves the body, especially if one happens to die in a high wind and not in calm weather.

Cebes laughed and said: "Assuming that we were afraid, Socrates, try to change our minds, or rather do not assume that we are afraid, but perhaps there is a child in us who has these fears; try to persuade him not to fear death like a bogey."

You should, said Socrates, sing a charm over him [*sic*] every day until you have charmed away his fears.

Socrates, *Phaedo*

The ethical self is an active relation between my actual self and a vision of my ideal self as one-caring and cared-for. It is born of the fundamental recognition of relatedness; that which connects me naturally to the other, reconnects me through the other to myself. As I care of others and am cared for by them, I become able to care for myself.

Nel Noddings

Chapter Three
INTERPRETING INTERPRETATION

No sensible man [*sic*] would insist that these things [about what is above the earth and below, and about the reward and hope of the soul] are as I have described them, but I think it is fitting for a man to risk the belief—for the risk is a noble one—that this, or something like this, is true about our souls and their dwelling places, since the soul is evidently immortal, and a man should repeat this to himself as if it were an incantation, which is why I have been prolonging my tale.

Socrates, *Phaedo*

All philosophers, accordingly, have conceived of the whole world after the analogy of some particular feature of it which has particularly captivated their attention.... Common men [*sic*] find themselves inheriting their beliefs, they know not how. They jump into them with both feet, and stand there. Philosophers must do more; they must first get reason's license for them.

William James

Chapter Four
PHILOSOPHIES OF OUR DAY

Are you not ashamed that you give your attention to acquiring as much money as possible, and similarly with reputation and honor, and give no attention or thought to truth and understanding and the perfection of your soul?

...For I spend all my time going about trying to persuade you, young and old, to make your first and chief concern not for your bodies nor for your possessions, but for the highest welfare of your souls, proclaiming as I go, Wealth does not bring goodness, but goodness brings wealth and every other blessing, both to the individual and to the state.

Socrates, *Apology*

One of the great liabilities of history is that all too many people fail to remain awake through great periods of social change.... Today our very survival depends on our ability to stay awake, to adjust to new ideas, to remain vigilant and to face the challenge of change.

Martin Luther King Jr.

Chapter Five
A VISION OF HUMAN MATURITY

...I have had a remarkable experience. In the past the prophetic voice to which I have become accustomed has always been my constant companion, opposing me even in quite trivial things if I was going to take the wrong course.

Socrates, *Apology*

Therefore the basic anxiety and self-estrangement inherent in human existence can never be overcome unless we first overcome the ego-self and awaken to our true Self.

But the true Self continually recedes, step by step, as we repeatedly ask about ourselves. This process is endless —it is an infinite regress. And yet, while increasingly compelled to engage in this endless process of grasping, we are also forced to realize that that which can be grasped is never anything more than an objectified, dead self.... No matter how many times we may repeatedly ask ourselves, our true Self. Always stands 'behind'; it can never be found in 'front' of us. The true Self is not something attainable, but that which is unattainable. When this is existentially realized with our whole being, the ego-self crumbles. That is, the existential realization of the unattainability of the true Self culminates in a deadlock, the breaking through of which results in the collapse of the ego-self, wherein we come to the realization of no-self or no-ego-self.

Masao Abe

Is it not true that the far-reaching adaptability to living a lie and the effortless spread of social auto-totality have some connection with the general unwillingness of consumption-oriented people to sacrifice some material certainties for the sake of their own spiritual and moral integrity? With their willingness to surrender higher values when faced with the trivializing temptations of modern civilization? And in the end, is not greyness and the emptiness of life in the post-totalitarian system only an inflated caricature of modern life in general?

Vaclav Havel

Chapter Six
PHILOSOPHICAL JOURNAL

Knowing ignorance is strength.
Ignoring knowledge is sickness.

Tao Te Ching
Number Seventy-One

Philosophy is the thought with which or as which I am active as my own self. It is not to be regarded as the objective validity of any sort of knowledge, but as the consciousness of being in the world.

Karl Jaspers

Chapter Seven
PHILOSOPHY, DEVELOPMENT, AND THE WORLD

Democratic pluralism, on the face of it a fine position, cannot be espoused in today's world as if all we had to do was *choose* it. To achieve a truly egalitarian pluralism conceptually and politically, it is necessary for all groups to achieve self-knowledge, developed from within rather than imposed from without.

Elizabeth Kamarck Minnich

We are at a critical juncture to move beyond three prevalent but outmoded exclusive dichotomies: the traditional/modern, the West/the rest, and the local/global.

Tu Weiming

CHAPTER TWO

DIALOGUE QUESTIONS

1. What is your response to the claim that reading, writing and the inclusive art of conversation are fundamental to the practice of philosophy?
2. What discipline have you developed for the practice of these arts, and how might it be improved?

Related to Chapter 1,

3. When have you experienced wonder/wisdom/vitality/ genuine self?
4. What have you been able to do (or not do) to make it possible for this experience to occur again or more broadly in your life?
5. What are the real questions, problems, issues for you?

CHAPTER THREE

INTERPRETING INTERPRETATION

"PHILOSOPHY," in its secondary and more limited sense, as articulation of what I am committed to and what I think I know, is inevitable. I speak of these things, for better or for worse, to both myself and others, whether I am an "intellectual" or not. Also inevitable is philosophy in its primary sense of the transformation process of examining and refining those commitments and thoughts over time. The question is not whether or not I have a philosophy or do philosophy, but only which one and with what degree of effectiveness I question and cultivate my philosophy. The question is not whether I move from one "philosophy" (and religious orientation) to another, but whether I do this in a mode of growth and development—or in a mode that reacts to threat, negativity, fear.

All philosophers, accordingly, have conceived of the whole world after the analogy of some particular feature of it which has particularly captivated their attention....Common men [*sic*] find themselves inheriting their beliefs, they know not how. They jump into them with both feet, and stand there. Philosophers must do more; they must first get reason's license for them.[32]

William James

No sensible man [*sic*] would insist that these things [about what is above the earth and below, and about the reward and hope of the soul] are as I have described them, but I think it is fitting for a man [*sic*] to risk the belief—for the risk is a noble one—that this, or something like this, is true about our souls and their dwelling places, since the soul is evidently immortal, and a man should repeat this to himself as if it were an incantation, which is why I have been prolonging my tale.[33]

Socrates, "Phaedo"

This chapter is a meditation on philosophy in the secondary sense: as the life-interpretation I have at this point in time, as the writings of other philosophers I encounter, and as the commitments I have made that give body to my life. It is a meditation on the human function of interpretation and the stuff of the "examined life," i.e., that which needs to be examined.

In the Christian New Testament (and various other world scriptures) we are challenged to become like little children, and like lilies and ravens that "neither sow nor reap."(Luke 12:24). They just are what they are. They act from a place within themselves that Robert Pirsig, in his contemporary *Zen and the Art of Motorcycle Maintenance,* refers to when he says "The silence allows you to do each thing right."[34] No hesitation. No hiddenness. No "philosophy" to get in the way. Fully spontaneous. Fully present. Fully the clear glass of Zen—or the "knowing nothing" of Socrates.

The point of these challenges is that we need to become like this. We are not there yet. Instead we are consumed with an awkward self-consciousness shaped by self-concern. We are in need of redemption, or discipline—some fundamental change or transformation.

The Greek origins of Western civilization present a distinctive view of the human awkwardness and what to do about it: the grandeur of human life arises from this very self-consciousness, from the fact that we are conscious. We are the form of life that transcends itself in such a way that we not only respond, but have responsibility; we not only re-act, but we act. Such key ethical words as "ought," "should," "freedom," and "will" all presuppose that we can stand above or go beyond our genetic programming and social conditioning—and even our "self" as it is identified in any moment (and in our "self image"). We can decide, promise, and live in communities ordered by constitution rather than force. We are capable of going beyond the conclusions, both intellectual and emotional, we have drawn from previous experience. We can be persuaded: we can stand outside of ourselves and learn, even become wise.

What to do in the interim between awkward self-consciousness and wisdom? Here is the anguish as well as the opportunity of human life. Here is where Socrates can help.

* * *

Again, we must be careful not to leap too fast to the "knowing nothing" stage that is ideal (or the "burning of the scrolls" stage in Buddhism). We must remain and be committed to the full work of philosophy in the secondary sense—as a subject matter to be "examined," as the "history of philosophy," and our own formulations, commitments and positions in life.

Speaking individually, our patterns of decision and action arise from our "philosophy," from the more or less conscious structure of value, meaning, and assumption that is integral to each person.

Another word for philosophy in this sense is "interpretation." We have experiences in life, and then we draw back into interpretation, into the evaluation and organization of experiences in an overall pattern of value and meaning, including rules, commitments, and other ideas that help orient us to fresh experience in the future. And, as William James points out in the statement at the beginning of this chapter, our interpretations of the whole arise from some feature or part of experience that has especially impressed us. Interpretation in this way unifies, while it appears that experience is by definition plural—multifarious, many, full of conflicting possibilities and actualities. Through interpretation we live "in the image of God," as creators, as beings capable of bringing order to chaos. One significant way that we do this is by using our interpretations to remind us of who we are when we are at our best. We "create" ourselves as well as our world.

It is a "natural" part of human life, then, to move back and forth between the freshness and adventure of immediate experience on one side, and the security and enclosure of interpretation on the other. Or, to switch the metaphor, humans quite naturally live out of interpretation because we need more in the way of a navigational system in life than is provided by genetics and conditioning. And this "more" is large: our interpretations must account for experiences of both awe in the universe and insufficiency in ourselves. They must be religious.

* * *

I have spoken of interpretations in terms of "values, meaning, and assumptions." The term "assumption" indicates that most human beings are aware of their interpretations only to a very limited degree. For the most part interpretations are unconscious, buried beneath awareness in unexamined assumptions about how life must be and what must happen. These patterns of assumption were imprinted on the person through preconscious childhood experiences, and they functioned deterministically—to eliminate the possibility of freedom and openness that comes with being fully present.

The Socratic genius lay in his ability to bring interpretation to consciousness in such a way that evaluation of one's interpretation becomes possible, along with the possibility of choosing a more favorable structure of interpretation (or "philosophy"). And with Socrates there is a developmental aspect, such that in the process of moving to better interpretation there are also moments of "knowing nothing," wonder, and truthfulness in which we have progressively greater access to our "inner voice" or authentic selfhood. The experience of this voice—which, paradoxically, is also that silence through which right action flows—is beyond all words; it is more like the source from which any interpretation arises than it is something that could be described. It is like the Tao that is described in the Chinese classic, the *Tao Te Ching:* "The Tao that can be told is not the eternal Tao; The name that can be named is not the eternal name."[35] Through repeated experience of coming to aporia—the Socratic realization of not-knowing—we learn to become like lilies and ravens; we learn to become human beings.

* * *

Yes, but. As a matter of fact very few human beings have actually engaged the Socratic practice with much rigor.—Despite the fact that human experience on this planet generally gives testimony to this process, whether we call it "philosophy" or not, we suffer repeatedly the "not knowing" or loss of that in which we had entrusted our existence, until we learn to trust that which is truly trustworthy. In order to appreciate the relative absence of Socratic practice in one sense, and its inevitability in another, we need some very broad perspective on the history of the human race. We need to become conscious of "our" common cultural relationship with philosophy in the traditional period of human history. This perspective could give us access to the benefits of Socratic practice in the present.

One of the amazing qualities of our times is that the entire history of humanity becomes available to us. From this perspective it appears that the whole of the Historical Period—from around 600 B.C. to sometime in the twentieth century[36]—was foundationalist or essentialist. This is to say that people were born, lived, and died within one community of interpretation or philosophy that assumed (in ways we would now find naive) that its interpretation was representative of the way things are, that the interpretation corresponded to reality itself. This understanding that one's interpretation was in direct correspondence with reality itself meant that all other communities of interpretation were understood to be either radically less right than we, or wrong—those others were heathens, pagans, primitives, enemies, or incarnations of evil.

In the history of Western culture, narrowness of closed community was made more severe by Judeo-Christian and Islamic notions of being chosen people, of being elected and enlightened through special revelation.

Severity of closed community and closed spirits was also encouraged by Greek intellectualism in the West. Intellectualism means that the function of interpretation is located mostly within the rational, logical mind, with little insight coming in either from experience "below" or from divinity "above." This orientation, sometimes called "logocentrism," came to be the dominant one in Western culture, if not by the time of Aristotle (d. 322 B.C.), then certainly by the time of Descartes (d. 1650). The effect was great advances in technology and enormous capability in satisfying the physical and psychological wants of human beings, but little nurture or development in the moral and spiritual dimensions. This had led to twentieth century discoveries of, in the words of Martin Luther King, "a poverty of the spirit which stands in glaring contrast to our scientific and technological abundance."[37]

Meanwhile, the Western orientation was exported all across the globe through "development," melting traditional cultures in its wake and unifying the globe. The world history of conflicts about whose interpretation was best or truly correct seems to have ended sometime between the Second World War and the Vietnam War and given way to competition in world markets and a new catholicism of consumption, entertainment, and management.

Interpretation, philosophy, meaning, religion, the humanities: they are not what they used to be. In the new authority, numbers are what matters: in polls, profit-loss calculations, outcome assessments, cost-benefit analysis. —And if not numbers, then "whatever," relativism, a mushy toleration that is cynical about any commitment.

World history of people living in isolated interpretations of "the One," and of conflicts with other cultures about whose interpretation was correct, has broken up. So far as we can tell, ours is a time between times, an interim period, a time "between the no longer and the not yet." Ours is in time, as Robert Bellah points out, where dualistic metaphysical worldviews have been replaced by a new view which is "infinitely multiplex."[38] It is a time of irony, historical consciousness, and contingency.

Several distinct orientations to the interpretive function itself (as distinct from the actual interpretations that prevail—which are discussed in Chapter 4) become visible. These orientations are also revealing of the moods or fields of feeling that characterize our era. Let me just describe very briefly several of the more prominent ones, and then conclude with the suggestion that out of the confusion and chaos of our time, the genius of Socrates becomes available to us more strongly than it had been for centuries, perhaps since the ancient intellectualism set in with Aristotle.

1. Sleep or numbness in the interpretive function; unwitting surrender to forces of consumerism, addiction to sensation. Materialism, cynicism, skepticism—"Whatever." People live shallow lives of busy-ness and entertainment. They skim across the surface, avoiding depth and real contact; they meet only on the flat ground of exchanging goods and services—emotional as well as physical—in a world of otherwise isolated individuals pursuing their self-interests. This orientation, which can be seen as a surrender of humanity itself, is perhaps understandable as a response to the enormous stress of a life-situation that is new, demanding, and disturbing.

2. Some are awake to the question of interpretation and claim that we are now freed from this function so we can return to the "Garden of Eden," the prehistoric dimension of the unconscious, to pure experience, the prephilosophical state of nature, just being.... Romantics, Bohemians, Beatniks, Hippies, Generation X (?); Phenomenology, Expressionism, Impressionism, Oriental acceptance, Existentialism. The urge to return to body wisdom, to celebrate the gift of quality of life itself. The problem here seems to be an overly simple view of human nature and ignorance of the difficult path of purification. As a result, we have premature claims to "know nothing," enlightment, wisdom, or to live out of "the silence that allows you to do each thing just right."

3. Some others agree with the claim that humans have evolved beyond interpretation, seeing the interpretations of traditional religion and culture as "opiates of the people" (Marx) or "illusions" (Freud). But these "secular" voices usually substitute another interpretation: that of social science. Sometimes the champions of this lifeway are not aware of science as itself an interpretation; they take their social science as simply representative of "the way things are," and in this respect they are ironically similar to the traditional cultures they so frequently look down upon.

The problem here, I think, is brilliantly described by Hans-Georg Gadamer. Since the philosophy of social science will be a major agenda item for the next chapter, I will just let Gadamer speak for himself at this point:

> By understanding the other, by claiming to know him, one robs his claims of their legitimacy. In particular, the dialectic of charitable or welfare work operates in this way, penetrating all relationships among men as a reflective form of the effort to dominate. The claim to understand the other person in advance functions to keep the other person's claim at a distance.... A person who does not admit he is dominated by prejudices will fail to see what manifests itself by their light. It is like the relationship between I and Thou. A person who reflects himself out of the mutuality of such a relation changes this relationship and destroys its moral bond.[39]

Social science becomes a form of "claim[ing] to understand the other person in advance," and hence violating the very humanity of others—and themselves (again, more on this in Chapter 4).

4. Fascism, cults, reactionary movements. The ambiguity and uncertainty, the insecurity, confusion, rapid change, and instability: these become too much for the human organism to bear, and a sort of reflex reaction occurs, a recoil from life in the present, into ideologies that fuse idealized senses of the past with fantastic visions of the future. The deep frustration of our time lays down a predilection for atrocity and terror—that frequently serve as the fusing agent. Diagnosis of this pathology is itself complex (Hannah Arendt once likened fascism to an onion: endless layers but no center).[40] It is enough at this point to simply remind ourselves that this possibility exists and to retake the vow to never forget.

5. Now we come to what I have been calling the Socratic possibility. This, as you know, is the possibility in our cultural moment that I want to illuminate from as many sides as possible throughout this book.

The Socratic possibility is visible from one of its sides within the hermeneutical orientation of our era, with its consciousness of interpretation itself as the human way of relating to truth. Gadamer, for example, in the passage just cited, reveals how greater awareness of the interpretive function can make it possible for us to choose ways of understanding that are conducive to full mutuality. David Tracy, to select another prominent example of the creative hermeneutical orientation, speaks of faithfulness to conversation: "...that unnerving place where one is willing to risk all one's present self-understanding by facing the claims to attention of the other. In any conversation we may find ourselves called to change either radically, as suggested by the religious language of conversion, or less completely but genuinely, as in any acknowledgment of the once merely different as now genuinely possible.[41] Real conversation becomes possible only when one is conscious of the interpretive function: conscious of the fact that I must *have* an interpretation, but also conscious that mine is not the only or final interpretation.

We also see the Socratic possibility in the American movement of pragmatism. Listen to William James in his famous essay, "What Pragmatism Means":

> You see by this what I meant when I called Pragmatism a mediator and reconciler and said, borrowing the word from Papini, that she 'unstiffens' our theories. She has in fact no prejudices whatever, no obstructive dogmas, no rigid canons of what shall count as proof. She is completely genial. She will entertain any hypothesis, she will consider any evidence...Her manners are as various and flexible, her resources as rich and various, and her conclusions as friendly as those of mother nature.[42]

Pragmatism, like the examined life of Socrates, is a way of living, one which must not be eclipsed by "philosophy" in the sense of final theories and intellectual formulation. Pragmatism is concerned with how modes of thought place us in life, whether in healthy or unhealthy ways. Pragmatism even suggests that some of the most important realities to us—like freedom, and love, and maybe even God—depend for their very ability to remain on this planet at least in part on the human willingness to believe in them.[43] Again, what we think is important, but it is relative to something still more important—like what Socrates calls "a life worth living."

And note that James refers to pragmatism as female![44] In the twentieth century we have discovered the "other" aspect of our humanity that had been repressed (and suppressed, and oppressed) in the Historical Period. This other is frequently spoken of in terms of the feminine dimension of existence. In the "Socratic" feminism of our era "the other" comes to be understood as the receptive or relational mode, and the ideal to be one of harmonizing or "caring" as the developed ability to move back and forth between two modes of human existence. Nel Noddings is especially clear on this:

> The receptive or relational mode seems to be essential to living fully as a person. In caring, a permanent or untimely move from feeling and affective engrossment to abstract problem solving would be a "degradation," a movement from the appropriate to something qualitatively different and less appropriate. Again, this is not to say that a lateral or temporary move into objective thinking is necessarily a "degradation." What seems to be crucial is that we retain the ability to move back and forth and to invest the appropriate mode with dominance. When we give control to the inappropriate mode, we may properly speak of a degradation of consciousness; in the one case we become irrational and in the other unfeeling and unseeing.[45]

Faithfulness to relationship of a conversational or democratic nature, as the kind of relationship in which humans thrive, makes it possible to envision the kind of human growth the world so urgently needs. Elizabeth Kamarck Minnich is eloquent on this: "...we stop confusing equality with sameness; we learn to think much more subtly and to live and work with more complexity and fineness of feeling and comprehension, taste and judgment. We begin again to create ways of thinking that support democracy rather than undermining it, as the old hierarchically invidious monism has done for so long."[46]

"The Socratic possibility": I am suggesting that this stream or energy within Western culture becomes available again in our time. It becomes available, after many centuries of eclipse by intellectualism, "abstract problem solving," and "hierarchically invidious monism." Availability occurs through the meeting with that which had been held off as "other" in the dominant orientation of the Historical Period. The "other" takes several forms, including the hermeneutical orientation, pragmatism, and feminism. Another powerful source of otherness through which recovery of the Socratic lifeway occurs is Eastern culture. Underneath the complexity of Eastern cultures there is a sense of the necessity of inner or mystical development, and the calm appreciation of the simple is-ness of what is. These qualities, along with the developmental methods that engender them, are badly needed in the West. They speak to the sort of human development that is required in order to appropriate the Socratic lifeway, a development that had been largely forgotten in Western education and child rearing—just as Western academics forget that Socrates must have meditated as a part of his examined life.[47]

Perhaps we can conclude this very brief discussion of that dialogue with the other through which the Socrates possibility becomes accessible again with a statement from the influential Zen spokesperson Masao Abe. Here is a very rich and large statement in which he ties together the feminine and Eastern influences, and suggests the same sort of integration that is pointed to by Nel Noddings and so many others in our time:

> We can be no more satisfied with mere paternalistic Christianity as an occidental form of world religion, than with mere maternalistic Buddhism as an oriental form of world religion. Both father and mother are needed to provide a real 'home' for us. Yet this should not be seen as only a mixture of Christianity and Buddhism. Christianity, we can see from its mystical tradition, is not totally lacking the maternal, receptive aspect, nor is Buddhism, judging from Nichiren, entirely alien to the paternal and justice-oriented aspect. However, neither in Christianity nor in Buddhism

> have these two essential aspects been thoroughly and harmoniously realized. But, to cope with the radically changing meaning of the 'world' and the resultant human predicament, Christianity and Buddhism must break through their respective occidental-paternal, oriental-maternal structures. Each must develop and deepen itself to achieve a universal form of world religion.[48]

* * *

Back to the immediate issues about interpretation with which this chapter began. There is no way for me, a human being, to be free of interpretation. For better or for worse, I will have one. But there are better and worse, and the historical consciousness of our time requires that I be, in the words of Robert Bellah, "responsible for our choice of symbol system."[49] This, of course, is an unthinkable proposition from the standpoint of our ancestors who were not conscious of their interpretations as anything other than statements of how things are. For most of them, interpretation was either right or wrong, and given, not chosen. Responsibility for my interpretation is equally unthinkable to the relativists of our day for whom the plurality of interpretations quickly becomes their equal irrelevance—the "equality of sameness" to which Minnich refers.

Responsibility for my interpretation both requires and induces growth between the "Catch 22" of the two orientations just described. It requires that I not identify totally with my interpretation, but see that my interpretation is relative to something larger, namely the life I live. Here is Socrates' point from the beginning of this chapter about the importance of "risking the belief" and repeating it to myself "as if it were an incantation": "no sensible person" can ask for guarantees of certainty in the matter of what we believe, therefore we have choice in this matter, a choice that makes a big difference in how we live. It is this very point that James radicalizes with his pragmatism, suggesting that we may actually play a part in the structuring of reality through our "will to believe." James is talking about something larger than just "my reality" in the contemporary psychological sense of "we all create our own reality." Rather, he is talking about reality itself, as indicated in the following statement: "Philosophies are intimate parts of the universe, they express something of its own thought of itself. A philosophy may indeed be a most momentous reaction of the universe upon itself."[50] The meaning of human beings as creators—or cocreators—begins to be more clear.

* * *

Perhaps we need to rediscover what we knew as children: that philosophy is the love of wisdom, not the possession of it. Rediscovering involves a certain humility, and acceptance of a paradox: that the only way for me to be free of the inevitable prejudices of *any* interpretation and to "know nothing" in anything like the manner of Socrates and other enlightened beings is to humbly accept the fact that I live through my interpretation (like the clothing Adam and Eve wore after they lost their innocence—or like the physical body in which I am incarnated). No matter how refined my interpretation may be, it cannot be the final interpretation. Creation continues....

Philo = love or friendship. *Sophia* = wisdom. Through the friendship of wisdom I am transformed as I accept the inevitability and (inevitable) limitations of my interpretation, I am in fact able to move toward knowing nothing (and to value those inexplicable, brief moments in my life when I truly am wise). In this movement I need to remember that the only wisdom Socrates claimed for himself was "a certain wisdom" that he called "human wisdom," consisting in his "not thinking that I know what I do not know."[51]

There are other claims of Socrates. He speaks of his "inner voice" and of the "prophetic voice" that has been his companion since childhood. The practice of philosophy certainly contains lessons in humility. But this is not all. The paradox of Socrates is that the "knowing nothing" is necessary to the turning around of the soul that makes it possible for us to know everything, to have access to the inner voice.

But we will never become "like lilies and ravens." For our species it always remains an open question as to whether we can become fully human. Ours is essentially a species in transition, in the process of becoming.

CHAPTER THREE

DIALOGUE QUESTIONS

1. What "philosophy," what interpretation or structure of value, meaning, and assumption, do you inherit from your preconscious childhood experience?

2. What philosophy have you chosen as an adult?

    a. How was it an "examined" choice?

    b. How does it relate to your imprinted philosophy?

3. How could your future choices of philosophy as life interpretation nurture a way of being in ordinary experience that is more loving, and more appreciatively aware, and more just?

CHAPTER FOUR

PHILOSOPHIES OF OUR DAY:

EASY-LIFE-ISM, MACHINE-ISM, AND THE PSYCHOLOGICAL WORLDVIEW

I FIND MYSELF LIVING IN THE MIDST of unresponsive people (sometimes me). Some live for sensation only, entertainment. They are never serious; often they are cynical, bringing down anything rising above the level of "fun." Others live as machines—cold, always calculating, always busy, always driving themselves and those around them. Neither type is really alive. Both have found ways to numb themselves to the depth dimension we had traditionally thought of as essential to being human. Both types lose the healthy open space between people (and within themselves), the first by fusing people into masses (as in mass entertainment, mass market, mass society), the second by driving them into isolation.

The psychological worldview of our era holds these two otherwise opposing types together, and supports them both. It can condone and legitimate both the fun orientation and the machine orientation. Psychology does this through objectifying self, taking the lead in the generalized denial of depth, and removing the open space of genuine encounter. In this way, the psychological worldview inevitably prescribes either selfish individualism or a determinism that eclipses responsibility and growth; either massification or isolation.

And yet the psychological worldview carries creativity and hope in our era also, serving that phase of human development in which we come to awareness of and healthy relationship with both self and other. None of us can exempt ourselves from the ambiguous and necessary work of psychology.

Are you not ashamed that you give your attention to acquiring as much money as possible, and similarly with reputation and honor, and give no attention or thought to truth and understanding and the perfection of your soul?

...For I spend all my time going about trying to persuade you, young and old, to make your first and chief concern not for your bodies nor for your possessions, but for the highest welfare of your souls, proclaiming as I go, Wealth does not bring goodness, but goodness brings wealth and every other blessing, both to the individual and to the state.[52]

Socrates, *Apology*

One of the great liabilities of history is that all too many people fail to remain awake through great periods of social change.... Today our very survival depends on our ability to stay awake, to adjust to new ideas, to remain vigilant and to face the challenge of change.[53]

Martin Luther King Jr., "The World House"

Given all that has been said above about the ambiguities of interpretation, this chapter is an attempt to practice the interpretive art.

Philosophy is practice of the examined life; it is identification and refinement of one's life interpretation, the at least partially conscious set of values, meanings, and assumptions that guide a human life. Philosophy makes it possible for us to move from interpretations that are unconscious, arbitrary, and dense to ones that are more conscious, chosen, and clear—allowing human beings to approach "knowing nothing" and genuine presence.

But nothing much is possible until we can admit that we have an interpretation, rather than simply The Truth, or a photographic representation of how things are. A major developmental threshold is crossed when we ourselves discover that we live through an interpretation that stands among other interpretations, at least some of which are seen as partially true. With this seeing we become capable of responsibility for our choices of life-interpretation, exercising the developed human capacity Elizabeth Minnich calls "reflexivity."[54] Nothing much is possible until we become aware of human otherness, including our own, developing sensitivity to the distinction between "my interpretation" and "me."

With this crucial discovery, we are ready to work with philosophy as a natural function of adult life, in the process of deconstructing and reconstructing our interpretations.

Here we also become aware of danger: we realize that barbarism—as the premature surrender to "flow" or "knowing nothing"—is what happens without philosophy, just as rigid orthodoxy or fascism is what happens with "too much" philosophy. We come to awareness that in any civilized setting the question is not whether or not philosophy, but whether people are able and willing to engage the examination process of dialogue through which human growth occurs.

* * *

In this chapter I want to venture a description of what I have come to understand as the three most prevalent life interpretations or philosophical orientations of our era, the third of which is also widely acknowledged as a source of remedy for distress within the other two. I call these "Easy-Life-ism," "Machine-ism," and "The Psychological Worldview."

* * *

But before diving in with my attempt to make these philosophies visible, I need to say just a few things about the ambiguities of the interpretive art in our time:

In the twentieth century we discovered that our very ways of describing are themselves part of our problem. Before we can speak, we must address the problem of speaking! This maddening circularity or inversion is at the root of the larger crisis of the humanities, which certainly includes philosophy. It accounts for much of the weirdness of twentieth century art and humanistic endeavor, including the urge to throw the viewer back on herself, to shock into wakefulness or at least a different frame of reference or "paradigm." It is not easy to live with reflexivity.

Also: we have become aware that our collective and "established" ways of describing have been determined and tainted by "logocentrism," "patriarchy," notions of racial and cultural superiority, and obsession with control: ways structured by reason, hierarchy, and absolutes rather than by relationships, events, and processes. Given the lenses they were wearing, it is no wonder that our Western ancestors were so curiously oblivious to the dynamics of human development and community, preferring the more simple either/or of inclusion/exclusion.

One way of describing the resultant problem with description, once the ambiguities of our past become more or less visible, is to say that Western culture lost confidence in the real, in our ability to make contact with reality, even belief in the existence of such a thing as "reality." Hence we live with postmodernist cynicism or relativism in relation to any interpretation. Nihilism, meaningless-ness, "whatever" are always nearby in our interactions today.

In the most positive expression of this condition, we become aware that the real is so complex that each of us is capable of perceiving only a fragment of it, leading to a pluralism in which we are open to dialogue with others as a way of mutual growth (more about this later). On the negative side there is the more cynical view that there is no such thing as "the real at all," but only the clashing struggles of human beings with different interests and powers, some who find talk of "the real" advantageous.

Another way of describing our problem with description: ordinarily we get descriptions that are overly objective—everything reduced to quantity and predictable rules of repetition; or else we get descriptions that are purely subjective—merely expressions of someone's feelings or interests. Eclipsed is the middle that is fundamental to art, philosophy, and healthy relationship or conversation: the objectivity that only arises from the particularity of unique moments and individual vision, and the subjectivity of such depth that it opens onto that which is universal and profoundly common to all. Gone is what the Greeks called *phronesis,* practical judgment, determinations of truth, beauty, and goodness that are both specific to the unique circumstances of real life, and yet at the same time more revealing of universals than any intellectual generalization could be.

How, then, are we to talk, to reclaim the vivid talk through which clarity, truth, and compassion will flow? How could one even begin to speak in any reliable way about "philosophies of our day?" Old-fashioned philosophy, so often secure in logic alone, deduction, objective certainty, will not do. Newer styles of pure confession and autobiography won't do either. One is too general, the other too specific; one too abstract, the other too concrete.

William James, meeting with this very dilemma, declared that he needed "to learn to think in nonconceptualized terms."[55] He meant that he needed to think in the sense of reflecting on experience, and his previous interpretations of experience, developing an approach that avoids the inherited tendency to drift away from contact with the actual, concrete world of living, breathing life. He wanted to avoid the drift into "vicious intellectualism" wherein strange things happen, such as people once identified as equestrians being unable ever to walk again![56] James avoided subjectivism by staying in touch with relationships in which people would question and critique his interpretations. His approach is narrative, anecdotal, eclectic; his approach is conversational.[57]

In order to speak truth with one another, we need a certain trust in the spontaneity of just what happens in encounter, in the act of communication in which truth is more an event and a kind of relationship than simply an intellectual object. Our approach must be experimental and improvisational rather than preparing everything beforehand! And it must be enjoyable, even playful (ludic)—though not in the way that is opposed to seriousness. Let me try a metaphor: Somehow we all need to stay in the kitchen and prepare the meal together (and perhaps the kitchen too!—and the building, the community, the world...), rather than treating the reader as the polite guest who must remain in the dining room, receiving only that which has been deemed fit to pass through a tightly sprung door.

It is with these thoughts in mind that I welcome you to the kitchen in which I work! Please help. Please engage in the dialogue with my own attempt to describe the actual philosophical orientations of our time. Please join me in a process of inquiry that is more like circling in on the matter at hand, rather than a strictly linear march to the conclusion of argument.

So here is the question: What interpretations do people actually live out of—or wear—today? What are the filters through which they experience and relate? In what follows, I share my attempt, in the newer mode of narrative and conversation, inviting your response. Anticipating your creative response, I can be bold in my own statement.

EASY-LIFE-ISM

The philosophy of Easy-Life-ism resists all description. It is Teflon-covered. It is "whatever." Traditional life-interpretations, whether cultural or personal, had an intellectual component, sometimes a doctrine, at least a recognizable set of beliefs or precepts. But the way of the Easy Life is to deflect, mock, or criticize away any interpretation. It is shiny, slick, evasive.

Let us try to catch the Easy Life in terms of the "structure of value, meaning, and assumption" (See Chapter 3) that make up a philosophy.

Another way to say that Easy-Life-ism is invisible to traditional categories is to say it is based in denial. Higher or deeper values? There are none. In fact, these things are best treated with ironic, postmodernist joking. Notice the number of popular movies that are based on visuals, "special effects," and music, and that are downright incoherent—even contemptuous—in the traditional terms of plot, meaning, character, relationship, and value. I recall having this response intensely, for example, in the movie *Batman*—a mere festival of special effects. Films like this both feed and reflect Easy-Life-ism, trading in sensation, surprise, and safe emotionality. They almost consciously refuse to "mean" anything.

As far as the traditional labels go, we are talking about Epicurianism, hedonism, ethical egoism, the self-interest of "objectivism" as Ayn Rand has (ironically) appropriated that term in her popular novels such as *Atlas Shrugged.*[58]

But these terms do not take us very far.

* * *

Bruce Wilshire expressed his frustration with the Easy Life as he encounters it in students by saying that "missing is any sense that anything is missing."[59] There is a vacuity, a vapidness, an absence; and these with both smugness and indolence—a sense that, as TV commercials like to point out, we "deserve" the life of privilege and luxury.

Moving in a little closer, as in moving toward a submerged object in muddy water, the Easy-Life-ism can be considered "whimpering," as in T. S. Eliot's famous lament: "This is the way the world ends, not with a bang, but with a whimper."[60]

The underlying distress or alienation of Easy-Life-ism gets to be about soul death. Soul apparently needs nourishment in order to remain and develop on this planet. And death of the soul in our time can seem so very pleasant.[61]

* * *

Easy-Life-ism begins in resignation tinged with resentment. There is a begrudging acceptance of loss: loss of possibility, enchantment, intimacy, vivacity.

Somehow the very structures of technology that were supposed to support individuals have turned on us. These structures now live lives of their own, quite beyond any human control. Things just happen. The natural world is ruined. The very forms of consciousness that gave us critical distance and liberation from older cultural forms now alienate us from everything. We are outside of everything—in outer space. Nowhere.

Everyone feels thwarted. Each seeks to claim the position of victim. Everyone claims more victimization than everyone else: the very word becomes a noun, a stuff, almost a currency for social exchange.

We take our sad revenge by refusing to thrive; having amputated hope and starved expectation, we turn away from possibility and openness to any higher or deeper sources of vitality. Think of it on the analogy of an eating disorder (recalling Franz Kafka's short story about "The Hunger Artist," one who starved himself in spiritual protest).[62]

One clever way to embody the masochism of this self-fulfilling prophecy of extinction is to appear to be doing the opposite: to party! (This word becomes a verb—a thing to do, a "lifestyle.")

There is no future tense. Thought of the future only makes you tense. So "chill out": don't think, "hang out." Be a little numb. "Have fun." (How often we say this to one another today. What do we mean?) Put on some music and "do" whatever substance puts you in the mood to just flow.

* * *

Flying to Japan to discuss a previous work, *Rediscovering the West,* I was caught up in the wonder of travel. I recall the delightful realization that the twelve-hour path of our 747-400 from Chicago, up and over the frozen north to Tokyo, was precisely the "Northwest Passage" that early European explorers of North America were looking for! How surprising the fulfillment of our dreams can be.

Other things happened on that flight:

I became aware of the person sitting next to me, Kana, a young Japanese college student who was going home after her year in Ohio at a liberal arts college. We chatted about summer plans, family, flying, and then moved on to more substantive matters. I asked her about the attitudes of young people in Japan, and she replied with some intensity that all they want is "the easy life." She said this as though she thought I would know what she meant.

We joked about the airline's hyping of its duty-free shopping service, referring to the perfumes and liquors displayed on the movie screen as cultic objects in the religion of consumerism. While she was making this comment I observed that the whole section of our plane was watching the movie screen on which images of these objects were projected (a little bit like Plato's cave); no one was reading or conversing or even looking out the window. We are such cooperative subjects. So reverent. So willing to watch the screen. Yet also how uncannily simple to find someone nearby who sees the same things I do.

(I continued to think about the temple quality of the whole experience, and began to wonder whether being in a temple or in the presence of the Holy for people in the traditional past might not be very much like our experience of flying to Japan. We are so enveloped by the experience, so totally subject to it, so absolutely contained.)

* * *

Yet people do break free of consumerism and the Easy Life. Kana and I spoke about flying. She spoke of her uneasiness, more with the thought of flying than the mechanics, the fact of our doing something we could not think (as opposed to the experience of ancestors who would think what they could not do). She spoke of her inability to comprehend that she was going from Ohio to her home in Osaka in one day. Here was communication at a different level from that of our easy banter about duty-free shopping—something more like communion.

I've experienced this event of communion with people before in the midst of the Easy Life, frequently as a surprising eruption. Sometimes right in a temple of consumerism or entertainment a deeper, more intimate aspect of the person will break through. It is as though it comes from under the Easy Life, and in my experience it always occurs in sharp distinction from the ethic of "having fun," which is integral to Easy-Life-ism. From the standpoint of this occasional revelation of genuine personhood or soul, it is hard not to see the Easy Life as one continuous distraction, as a matrix of pulsing noise, flashing image, and animal urge that specifically distracts us from ourselves as well as from awareness of the underlying offense to our humanity of a world structured by consumerism and technology. Like nitrous oxide in the dentist's office, the cadence of Easy-Life-ism causes us not to notice—to live in a perpetual state of amnesia.

People immersed in Easy-Life-ism are usually uncomfortable being alone—and uncomfortable also with any deep contact with others. The Easy Life is a sort of frozen middle, a "normal" or "ordinary" state where, despite loud music, not much is going to happen.

I guess I've also seen the limits of the Easy Life in a peculiar sort of boredom that shows up around its edges, in a sense that there must be more to life than all this bodily stimulation. I've seen the limit too in looks of resentment or envy—when people realize how arbitrary money is as the primary way of distinguishing people in the society of the Easy Life, or when they realize that "having fun," whatever else that phrase might or might not mean, is not something we can simply acquire.

On the theme of envy as fundamental to the life we share in this culture, I think Richard Stivers is brilliant: He points out that envy arises out of a particular kind of "reflection" that he (along with Kierkegaard) finds typical of our era, as the abode or internal residence of people—where they live. This state of being or place within lies in an unhappy middle ground between action in the world on one side and deep personal commitment on the other. Stivers describes it as "ruminating" on possibility, with envy and resentment arising out of this condition—like gases arising out of a bog. Let Stivers speak for himself:

> Reflection itself, Kierkegaard maintains, is not the problem, but rather reflection that does not result in action, reflection that becomes an escape from action. When reflection is not accompanied by inward moral commitment, envy ensues. The powers of reflection are at the disposal of selfish desires. One envies others, their possessions and accomplishments. "Selfish envy" actually deters the individual from decisive action; instead time is spent ruminating about one's possibilities or what it would be like to be someone else. At this point Kierkegaard draws a startling conclusion about the modern reflective and passionless age: "envy is the negative unifying principle." This envy has both individual and collective manifestations, for the envy within the individual has its counterpart in the envious attitudes of others....
>
> When the envy that is present in reflection as aesthetic possibility is not punctuated by decision and action, it spills over into moral ressentiment [envy]. Assuredly ressentiment is present in every age but what makes it different in the modern era is "leveling." By this Kierkegaard means the attitude that no one is better than I am. Because of a lack of moral character the individual denigrates and even ridicules those who have distinguished themselves. It is not enough to admire and envy the other; one must tear him down.[63]

With this statement we are back to the themes of denial and mocking with which we began discussion of Easy-Life-ism. The key, it seems—the bottom line, is a perverse kind of activism that issues out of what initially appears as a passive position. It is as though the "laid back" qualities of Easy-Life-ism violate something deep in human nature, a transcending or actualizing urge, something that must find expression as protest if not as glory.

Easy-Life-ism critiques and consumes everything, including itself. This is to say that there comes a time when one must either move on as a conscious act, or go under—into the oblivion of dis-ease. Easy-Life-ism cannot sustain itself.

MACHINE-ISM

I would like to write. I would like to live a life that honored writing and reading. But I have no time or space to write. And for the same reasons no one really reads anymore anyway.

The world is so full of task and busy-work, endless duties and lists. If you want to be active in the world as it is structured today, then you are overwhelmed, treating yourself more like a machine than a human being. I live by my lists, giving myself assignments, then carrying them out. There are things to be done to the point where human contact can be bothersome, an interruption. I am trained to prefer voice mail and e-mail to conversation; they transfer the information and task, skipping the ambiguity and possibility of real encounter. I learn to live "multiple tasking," addicted to task, not knowing what to do with myself apart from having a task—and threatened by or afraid of the open space of real life.

(I have a European friend who is quite persuasive in his understanding that America is in an advanced state of hysteria.)

Our admiration of machines, our worship of them, has extended way beyond "labor-saving devices." The machine has become a primary role model for people today. It has become the image, whether consciously held or not, of effective presence in the world. And our worklife with machines has become life, with the other stuff—like child rearing and family life generally, along with life as a citizen—becoming either a distressing distraction or an entertainment. Mechanism has crossed over from serving human life to usurping human life, preempting, overshadowing. We live in what Vaclav Havel describes as "the global automatism of technological civilization."[64]

Let me clarify what I mean by "machine," beyond the simple physical sense of the term, as it leaps the gap from physical to social reality. I mean a certain kind of rationality that is closely associated with mathematics, and that expresses itself in the human world as the urge to standardize all interactions and streamline them according to rules of outcome assessment. And the most general rules of assessment are those of efficiency and profit, such that procedure and management replace authority and leadership, within bureaucracy—which Hannah Arendt describes as a new form of government that emerges in the twentieth century, defined as "the rule of nobody."[65] Personal responsibility becomes obsolete.

The quiet coup of bureaucracy descends on the world of

human affairs gently, like a net. But then it tightens as it settles into every crevice of community, doing its work of identifying the standard function that is or should be performed in that particular place, and streamlining performance to eliminate anything extraneous. All open space is eliminated, all space in which creativity, thought, and human encounter might occur. Everything is rationalized; everything is objectified.

The reason I don't write is: meetings and memos, assessment procedures and evaluation processes, unit self-studies, faculty reviews, budget studies, affirmative action reports, a "reorganization task force," and curriculum committee forums... and lectures and other public events planned by colleagues who cannot come to the events I plan because they are exhausted from their own, even as I do not go to theirs because I am too busy planning or recovering from mine!

* * *

Society overall has gone through a tremendous movement away from the ambiguous mixture of enchantment and unexamined privilege that had prevailed in the Traditional Period, and toward the rationalization of everything. Efficiency, profit, and bureaucracy—these came to be the prevailing and directive forces. "Management" came to be the architectonic discipline, the priestly order of a new "celibacy of the intellect" through which, as Whitehead says, "The specialized functions of the community are performed better and more progressively, but the generalized direction lacks vision."[66]

And these forces, inherent perhaps in the modern experiment with individual freedom from the beginning, drive us to the extreme Catch 22 between quality and equality, and to the dim awareness that everything, including education and medical care, is slipping down to a low common denominator which itself becomes lower as the years pass. The modern freedom results in a new kind of bondage.

The radical nature of this cannot be emphasized enough. Ignorance of the impact of management causes people to become locked in frenzied and destructive debate about solutions that cannot possibly be effective, and that, in any case, do not begin to address the real problem. Vaclav Havel, the world citizen and playwright from Czechoslovakia, is one of the most acute diagnosticians of our condition. He speaks of ours as a "post-totalitarian system" of near total automatism that arises because of "the general unwillingness of consumption-oriented people to sacrifice some material certainties for the sake of their own spiritual and moral integrity."[67] Perhaps George Soros is pointing to the same reality when he says that, with the collapse of the Soviet Union, capitalism is the most dangerous threat in the world today.[68]

* * *

Instead of doing nothing, as in the Easy Life, in Machine-ism I overdo. I take up the position of manager in relation to myself, then drive myself as hard as any machine.

THE PSYCHOLOGICAL WORLDVIEW

Underlying the two philosophies already described in this chapter, there is a third: the Psychological Worldview. It lies under both Easy-Life-ism and Machine-ism, since both acknowledge psychology as a remedy for problems or dysfunction. "Psychological Worldview" (hereafter PW) refers to the new catholicity of social science that has emerged in the twentieth century, a popularized form of the broader movement of psychology in our era. The PW is so pervasive that it is taken to be universal, simply representative of the way things are. As with any catholicity, it becomes invisible.

The Psychological Worldview claims the legitimacy of science, and it arises out of the frequently conflicting claims of the social sciences. The PW scientizes: it is a strategy of adjustment and development that adds the authority of science to what is not science at all, except in the loosest ways—and except for the fact that the Psychological Worldview, like science, works by objectifying everything.

The basic characteristics of the PW reflect and extend the Western individualism out of which it arises. Let me attempt a compact description of these characteristics in a summary way:

> In relation to the other, an orientation to diagnosis and the reduction of persons and relationships to their problems; from the side of the one diagnosing, a legitimated retreat from the immediacy or "body" of lived life and relationships, into the enclosure of the intellectual construct of the diagnosis, and a subsequent refusal to acknowledge what is actually happening in real life; a tendency to uncritical or ideological preference of certain preestablished diagnoses, such as repressed memory of childhood abuse; a suspiciousness about anything or anyone associated with "higher" or "fully human" values, and a particular urge to focus the reducing force of diagnosis on this sort of claim whenever it appears; the presumption of isolated individualism, regarding virtually any relationship as among those "higher" realities; the denial of growth, development, or real learning; the assumption of competition and clashing self-interest as how the world really works; the need and the appropriateness of assertiveness skills as a remedy for exclusion, victimization, or marginalization in the past. Finally, from the larger world perspective, it must be said that the deep danger of the PW lies in the following: it is unconscious as to its own imperialism—in its very zeal to identify and deconstruct other imperialisms; its insistence on "multiculturalism" and "diversity" masks its underlying assumption of superiority (as though accusing the other of the very thing you are doing provides a good hiding place from which to launch the assault).[69]

* * *

I will now slow down and attempt to "unpack" this statement:

The Psychological Worldview, as I have said, is profoundly ambiguous: On the one hand it is helpful, even necessary at a certain stage of human development, a psychological stage that both marks a particular moment in human development and also becomes an ongoing hygiene that is necessary to healthy living. This I discuss in the next chapter, on the vision of human development and maturity that becomes available to us today, a vision that cannot even be seen until/unless one has done sufficient psychological work.

The other side of the ambiguity is that the PW, if it is not transcended and embraced within a larger and more adequate vision, worldview, spirituality, or philosophy, obliterates our humanity through its inherent activity of pro-jecting and objectifying. In the process of psychological investigation, what I was before is made other to me. Since that which is other is that in relation to which I may choose, I have the opportunity in the psychological process of becoming freed from what I was before—my problems, social conditioning, etc. But I also come into the condition Albert Camus, the great existentialist, describes so well as the experience of walking into a room containing nothing but your own dead body. If I am not ready for the identity crisis that lurks "under" most counseling, therapy, and analysis, then I am vulnerable to the nihilism of our era—or else mere facilitating, "enabling," or adjustment in Easy-Life-ism or Machine-ism. Philip Rieff indicates the danger of the historical emergence of "the therapeutic": "...with nothing at stake beyond a manipulatable sense of well-being. This is the unreligion of our age, and its master science.... The systematic hunting down of all settled convictions represents the anti-cultural predicate upon which modern personality is being reorganized, now not in the West only but, more slowly, in the non-West."[70]

But I am ahead of myself, into the end of this chapter and part of the next. I need to continue with the attempt to simply describe the PW. As I venture into this effort I recall Hannah Arendt's comparison of fascism to an onion: endless layers, but no center.[71] I think this is the point Camus and many artists in our time are trying to make about Nihilism.

* * *

First, within the PW there is orientation to problem and negativity. In any relationship a sort of scanning is immediately set in motion, searching the personality of the other or the social situation in which encounter occurs for areas of difficulty, dysfunction, or pain. Once identification of a problem has been achieved, there is rapid abstraction from the person or situation into a realm of diagnostic knowing where an interpretation is constructed. They—these people of the PW—always know, not only that you have some pain or grief, but the why and wherefore, and what must be done by way of remedy. Frequently the knowing is legitimated by theories associated with science or social science, but not necessarily. Diagnosis is given, and in some ways is ideally given, by assertion of the knower alone, as the expression of her superiority. Given the filminess of social science, there is a great deal of room in this orientation for a sort of politicizing of reality—and hence for lying and manipulation of the other according to the unexamined interests of the therapist. This occurs by way of assertion, and a certain "realism" about what is taken as an underlying human self-interest or "will to power." Lying also occurs out of a partial and preliminary understanding of "the social construction of reality" (i.e., the creative power of human beings to literally participate in the godly action of ongoing creation). The problem with therapeutic knowing, in Socrates' terms, is that it is not "fastened down" to true knowing, and hence is unstable.[72]

Seizing the high ground of knowing has the effect of reducing the other in their wholeness to an identified problematic part, reducing them to "their problem," and also of turning them from a subject into an object while at the same time moving from a relationship of mutuality to one of authority, from partnership to dominance. This move out of the sacred space of mutual relationship occurs in the form of James' "vicious intellectualism": once the conclusions of diagnostic knowing are achieved, there is refusal to consider further the actual case, the actual person. The relationship, in this sort of materialism of feelings and diagnostic ideas, must run one way only: from theoretical conclusions to the person or situation to which they apply, never the reverse. Here, it seems we have the Western Cartesianism at its extreme: the radical separation of mind from body, and the nearly fanatical preference for the former over the latter.

The diagnostic knowing immediately becomes both weapon and shield. As weapon, the knowing serves to control the other, and specifically to suppress or muffle them. The PW is literally depressing. For the diagnosis offered always places the knower in the superior position, and the known is taught first to identify with their problem, and second to submit to the treatment plan offered by the knower—which may simply be submission.

As shield, diagnostic knowing of the other serves to prevent intimacy or any deep human contact. Here is a major motive that is frequently difficult to see, because the social scientist will often appear vigorous in relationship, even confrontational. But the very "in your face" approach can be the most clever way to protect vulnerability and hide!

There is, then, frequently despite or under an interest in "therapy," a profoundly antirelational quality, a suspiciousness about relationship and a generally negative manner of relating that serves to confirm the suspicion—and enforce it. There is also, despite much talk to the contrary, an inherent denial of growth and development: once objectified, change, learning, real growth—as human possibilities of a genuine self emerging from the egg of ego—are impossible; lifelong learning—or any significant learning of a deep sort—is impossible. In the words of Doris Lessing, we inevitably become a "nothing but," to ourselves as well as others.[73] In its pervasive and tacit refusal of human development, the PW is located on the side of "determinism" rather than "freedom"; in the age-old distinction between these poles, now expressed as "diagnosis" versus "development," the PW can be seen to favor "behaviorism" as opposed to the "humanistic" movement in psychology.

In fact, this worldview is expressive of disappointment, a radical lowering of horizons, a sense of reduced possibility, frequently in the name of "realism." Here there is unhappy resignation to the circumstance in which whatever magic or enchantment or love may have once been on the Earth is now gone (or unmasked as someone's fantasy or way of manipulating children so they would sleep or behave). In the PW it is not realistic to hope for much, and not really possible for human beings to act in any way other than in their own self-interest—except, perhaps, pathologically against their self-interest, but in any case not for anything "higher" or beyond interest. Certainly terms of relationship beyond power and negotiation are impossible.

But as soon as the layer of disappointment is peeled off the onion of PW, a deeper layer is revealed. This is the mood of resentment and envy discussed earlier in relation to Easy-Life-ism, the wish to tear down and destroy, the wish to level down to the least common denominator. Here is the blind anger and enmity of our era, the lashing out, the orientation described so well by Nietzsche in his famous last sentence: "Mankind would rather will the void than be void of will."[74]

Finally, we come to that void itself, the centerless center. And here—within the frame of the PW—there are only questions: Could it be that this void is where the soul resided before? Has the soul departed, such that we have soulless flesh and ego active in our midst, totally "decentered" selves? Were "soul" and "self" only fictions that made it possible for people to get through the night in the past, or manipulate the masses? Has the soul suffocated and died; or has it had insufficient structure or housing in our period of rapid change and family instability, so it has simply blown away?

I know of no one who brings these questions into more sharp focus than Ira Progoff:

> Although it began as part of the protest against religion, the net result of modern psychology has been to reaffirm man's experience of himself as a spiritual being. Despite its conscious intention, the discipline of psychology recalls the modern man to an awareness of his inner life, thus reestablishing the ancient religious knowledge that man's fundamental accomplishments began within himself. This is a paradoxical outcome of Freud's work, and it has the broadest implication for our time.
>
> If psychology would fulfill its purpose in history, it must create with its own tools of analysis a practical means of transcending itself. Now it has come to a crossroads; but if we can judge from the mature, reconsidered works of its basic authors, the choice before it is clear. It must take the path that goes directly through the paradox underlying psychological work until, facing itself, it will ultimately fulfill itself by leading the "modern man in search of a soul" to a soul beyond psychology.[75]

The "beginning within" that is necessary to move toward "a soul beyond psychology" must certainly get past obsession with diagnostic knowing, especially since this obsession is at the root of the deadly objectification of other. This morbidity of the PW is crucial: In contemplating the consequences of objectification, it helps to recall that the distinction between treating someone as a subject rather than as an object is the most basic wellspring of Western ethics: that the other should always be treated as an end in themselves, never as a means; as a person rather than a thing, a thou rather than an it. In this respect, the PW can be seen as profoundly unethical.

But maybe, looking at it again, obsession with the superiority of "knowing," the tyrannical knowing that is fundamental to the PW, is not the root. Perhaps at the bottom of the new catholicity of the PW is a fear or inability to tolerate the open space of genuine human encounter. This space, of course, is also the space of soul. Here, as in the previous scenario as well, we are driven into the absence of open space that constitutes nihilism—emptiness that is filled with our own dread, the abyss of not knowing that is so frightening when it first appears.

It is only in that space "beyond psychology" that we can resolve the riddle of the PW considered as a developmental stage: "love yourself," or have "self-esteem." For it is only genuine self that could possibly appreciate and care for the very finite selves of endless ego and anxiety that are always there, like "the poor ye shall always have with ye" in Jesus' statement. Otherwise we teeter back and forth between arrogance and masochism.

CHAPTER CONCLUSION:

Machine-ism will sometimes present itself as remedy for the boredom that can infiltrate Easy-Life-ism, or as an antidote to the dangers of disappearing into addiction to more and more sensation. Machine-ism teaches us to focus, commit, make myself definite—"get a life!" In like fashion, Easy-Life-ism will sometimes present itself as the cure for the tedium of Machine-ism. It teaches us to relax, flow, "get over your problems with control." Psychology can relate to either problem and endorse either solution. For on one side of psychology the behaviorist schools treat the unruly subjectivity and body-character of humans in Easy-Life-ism. It does this by insisting that we are complex machines, bundles of stimulus-response conditioning—and treating accordingly. And on the other side, the existentialist schools correct for the overly objective and mind-oriented aspect of Machine-ism by helping us loosen up and surrender to the Hindu sense that everything happens just as it must.

Psychology in our era is similar to the Sophism in the ancient cultural environment of Socrates. It is not defined by any doctrine or agreement; it is more an attitude and a method, an attitude of adjustment and accommodation; it rarely critiques injustice, but instead prescribes the generalized "empowerment" of American culture and teaches us to adapt. At a deeper level the attitude is cynical in that nothing higher than success in whatever society one might find oneself in is envisioned. In this sense it is interesting to know that historical Greek Sophism has been referred to as a "social science."[76]

Western culture, especially since the time of Descartes at the beginning of the Modern Period (around 1650), has had problems with separating mind from body and leaving spirit out altogether. What is relevant from this long and complex story to us in understanding the philosophies of our day is that we are perpetuating an old problem: Easy-Life-ism is body separated from and even distainful of mind; Machine-ism is mind separated from—and distrustful of—body; and both, in their separation from the other, exclude spirit, meaning higher or deeper energies that might be brought to effective presence in the realm of human affairs. In this sense both Easy-Life-ism and Machine-ism are culturally arrogant, or blasphemous: they deny transcendence.

The psychological orientation of our era fails to go beyond the mind-body split that has troubled Western culture for so many centuries. And worse. The Psychological Worldview embraces the split and even provides a bridge on which to move back and forth from one side to the other. In psychology's embracing of the problem without solving it or going beyond it, a kind of hiding or even bad faith (in French, *mauvaise foi)* often occurs. Yet at the same time psychology also offers a platform from which transcendence can and does occur—as Progoff and others point out.

Bodies without minds. Minds without bodies. Nondoing without doing. Doing without nondoing. Romanticism versus classicism. Cooptation versus separatism. Dilemma/Catch 22/either-or/double bind/antinomy. Western culture encountering the abyss.

It is no wonder so many people in our century cite Proverbs 29:18: "Where there is no vision the people perish." Where is the vital middle, the resting point, the vision? Where is compassionate acceptance? ...Where is vigorous action?

...And what might it mean to say that none of us can be exempt from the necessity of psychology, that on its positive side it offers great opportunity? (See the last line of the summary statement at the beginning of this chapter.) With this question we move to the topic of the next chapter: human development, maturity, enlightenment.

CHAPTER FOUR

DIALOGUE QUESTIONS

1. Are the three philosophies described in this chapter indeed the most prevalent ones in your world?

2. How does your philosophy relate to each of the three philosophies described? What is your critique of each? What do you accept from each of the three philosophies discussed as a critique of your own life interpretation or philosophy—or at least as a suggestion about a dimension of experience to which you might pay more attention?

CHAPTER FIVE

ANOTHER POSSIBILITY

PHILOSOPHY AND HUMAN DEVELOPMENT

I GROW. I LOOK BACK at how I related and how I thought in the past, and see immaturity in relation to where I am now. I have developed, have learned, evolved. Philosophy helps in this. It has helped me be aware of dangers such as those of Easy-Life-ism, Machine-ism, and Psychological Worldview. Philosophy continues to help me remain alert and responsible in the movement from childish views to the "clear glass" view spoken of in Zen and other great traditions. It helps me identify my best moments of action and relationship in a way that makes possible a movement from those moments as extraordinary to becoming more ordinary. It helps me be aware of the progression itself, from childishness to maturity. Philosophy, as a developmental practice, helps me move through and beyond the necessary developmental task of psychology. Philosophy helps me move beyond both "psychology" and "philosophy."

I have had a remarkable experience. In the past the prophetic voice to which I have become accustomed has always been my constant companion, opposing me even in quite trivial things if I was going to take the wrong course.[77]

Socrates, *Apology*

To make his student face himself Socrates shows him the hopeless perplexity, the "aporia" or position with no way out, in which his ordinary muddle-headed notion about the truth would land him if its implications were worked out. Then he stimulates him gently to discover the right solution. In a similar way a Zen master tries to make his disciple face himself, to get him to return to the root-source of his being, by showing him a kind of "aporia" in which his analytical reason and intelligence come to a deadlock that can be overcome only by the awakening of his original nature. A Zen master, however, does so more severely than Socrates did.[78]

Masao Abe

Is it not true that the far-reaching adaptability to living a lie and the effortless spread of social auto-totality have some connection with the general unwillingness of consumption-oriented people to sacrifice some material certainties for the sake of their own spiritual and moral integrity? With their willingness to surrender higher values when faced with the trivializing temptations of modern civilization? And in the end, is not greyness and the emptiness of life in the post-totalitarian system only an inflated caricature of modern life in general?[79]

Vaclav Havel

This chapter, with the previous one which it continues, is an exercise in the art of interpretation.

What is more important to us today than human development?! What is more urgent—given the technologies at the disposal of human beings and the tenuously interdependent character of life on the planet? What is more significant in terms of our individual health and well-being, our abilities to cope with "stress" and generally live a vigorous and effective life in these incredible times?

Whether in personal or collective dimensions, what more basic fact of life is there than this?: that human beings must develop into beings that are more alert and more compassionate or else we will cause our own demise—one way or another—at great cost to other life forms on this planet as well. The suggestion of a new and expanded maturity is basic to our era; perhaps it is what keeps us from despair.

Indeed, one of the most promising discoveries of our time is that there is life after age twenty-one! There is available to us a vision of human maturity associated with life span development. We are liberated from that vast and uncharted plateau of "adulthood" on which most of our parents languished after they achieved majority, a way of making a living and a family. Right in the midst of the resignation and reduction of our era, a higher (or deeper) expectation also emerges. Martin Luther King, for example, speaks of a "revolution of value," in which people move from a "thing-oriented society" to a "person-oriented society."[80] Karl Jaspers describes the emergence of "a new nobility" of "self-existent selves,"[81] and Vaclav Havel points to an "existential revolution" through which people develop a new way of thinking that enables them to "live in truth."[82] Carol Gilligan speaks of a "vision of maturity" in which men and women learn to be both independent and intimate simultaneously.[83]

But the vision of a more mature, more fully developed human life form is only available to us in fragments. We may see and be inspired by it through a movie or a novel, but then it fades away, into the abyss of the huge amount of dramatic impressions that pass through us each day. We may glimpse this same vision of maturity through a hero, or through the genuine presence of a friend or even a stranger who walks through our life, but then the tide of alternating busyness and "fun" washes over us. We may even experience maturity firsthand in our own lives, in our best moments. But this is difficult to sustain in a world of entertainment and task, in a kaleidoscope society of flashing images and endless changes of subject.

In this chapter I want to share the sense in which dialogue with Socrates can help us put together and integrate our occasional glimpses of human maturity—in a way that helps us live this vision rather than just think it or admire it when it appears out of nowhere in our lives.

Here I present a fourth philosophy: one beyond the relativism of Easy-Life-ism, the absolutism of Machine-ism, and the soullessness of the Psychological Worldview. I want to present a philosophy that is oriented to development, and one I recommend as reliable for our very practical purposes of living a life. To give a name to this fourth orientation, let us call it Developmental Philosophy. My hope for this chapter is to simply provide some articulation of a vision that is already familiar to many of us, though so often only in fragments or brief glimpses. To be clear—what I am saying is that the "Developmental Philosophy" is present and active in our culture today, widely available, and not too difficult to understand.

Returning to Socrates' originating understanding of philosophy, we can see that philosophy is less about the holding of any particular idea than it is a practice through which human maturity develops. Out of the dialogue with Socrates, I present the emerging vision of adult development in four stages: psychological, intellectual, spiritual, and historical.

But right away we should be cautious about generalizing, not to mention compartmentalizing or presupposing a simple linear pattern. (I recall at this point the sad story of some nurses who inadvertently violated a dying person and their family by insisting that they must progress in the "right" order through Elizabeth Kubler-Ross's famous five stages of death and dying!)[84] As is evident from our experience with people we know, the most surprising things can occur in the drama of our movement to maturity: some can be more developed in "higher" spiritual stages, as though they were born that way, while relatively undeveloped in "lower" psychological stages; some meet with trauma that induces a leap in one aspect of their being or a regression to an earlier phase; some become arrested or deflected, trapped and overdeveloped in one stage where they may remain for a whole lifetime. And there is the suggestion that movements to maturity tend to be different in men and women.[85] With humans, surprise and diversity are to be expected!

And yet. It remains the case that there are more and less developed forms of human life, and that there is such an identifiable, recognizable phenomenon as maturity. It perhaps offends our American egalitarian sensibilities to say it is still the case that "the higher knows the lower, but the lower does not know the higher" (sometimes offending to the point that people give up on parenting, for example—or worse yet, ask their children to parent them!). But of course, it all depends on what the scale might be. A scale that defines nobility in terms of human development is vastly different from both the old aristocracy of blood and the newer aristocracy of mere money.

Still, as Hitler and others have reminded us, notions of a more developed form of human life can be dangerous. And, no matter how it is specified, "development" cannot be equated with "better"; the more highly developed life forms are also the ones capable of greater damage, tragedy, and evil. It is this last crucial point that the great traditions affirm by saying that *prajna* (wisdom) is *karuna* (compassion); or that, as in Platonism, returning to service in the world is the culmination of human experience of the Good; or that, in the Christian words of Dietrich Bonhoeffer, "Being there for others is the experience of transcendence..., a new life in 'existence for others,' through participation in the being of Jesus."[86]

So with these qualifications I proceed to offer a view of the emerging vision, and the suggestion of synergy between this vision and Socrates—such that each illuminates the other. This is what I mean by earlier claims about Socrates becoming available to us today in a way that has not been possible for a long time.

PSYCHOLOGICAL DRAMA

Over the entrance to the Oracle at Delphi were printed these words: "Know Thyself." I recall remarks by Albert Einstein and other great people to the effect that overcoming the self is the most profound challenge in life. Yet overcoming the self cannot mean leaving the self, and neither can it mean identifying with the self. The process is subtle and complex; it is something like a camel passing through the eye of a needle—that is, something that is "impossible" from any standpoint outside of the process.

The process begins in those moments when we awake from the dreaming innocence of childhood to discover: I am. We become conscious of ourselves, to the fact of our existence, to the definiteness of our selfhood against the backdrop of the whole wide world and the starry heavens.

At first it may be romantic, this self-consciousness, or narcissistic; a burst of self-love that may serve to propel a full movement out of the childhood state of nature onto the plain on which the drama of knowing self is to occur.

A short time later, greater differentiation from self occurs, such that we can begin to speak of self-concept and self-image, adopting a good attitude and positive thinking, etc. It begins to be possible to examine the awareness of self that I have, to see it as positive or negative, and to imagine a therapy of change. Here appeal can be made to maintaining self-respect or taking care of myself—as well as to growing up!

A little later, and frequently after some frustration in efforts to deal with the self in the mode just mentioned, we begin to make the acquaintance of what Socrates called "the frightened child within." We also discover the necessity that Socrates spoke of in terms of the need to "say a magic spell over him [*sic*] every day" until we have "charmed his [*sic*] fears away."[87] Knowing thyself becomes a matter of understanding the child, its fears and desires, and its sweet side as well. Here we encounter self as other.

The presupposition and reason for therapy at this stage is much like that of liberal education: that through conscious awareness, bringing into the light of day, I work against the determining influence of previous experiences, and that through this pro-jection (literally, throwing out) or objectification (making other) I have new choices about how and who to be. I have learned, in the words of Robert N. Bellah, "the laws of the self's functioning," and to be responsible for myself.[88]

Knowing myself as a "frightened child" is extremely helpful. Humans naively take their childhood experiences, some quite painful or strange, to be revelations of how things are in all of life. We do this in the deep tissues of selfhood which are formed in preconscious existence. What else could we do, since I had no environment external to my own experience? But through adult therapy and the miracle of objectification I see that my own experiences need not be determinative. In fact, if I can remain alert as to the conditioning, habits, and reflexes that were established in childhood (or perhaps previous lifetimes—I really do not know), I can choose to do otherwise in the adult present. I can be aware of new situations that are likely to engage the old patterns, and consciously choose to act contrary to those patterned behaviors. And I can reveal the ways in which I am wounded and flawed to those who care about me, so that they can help me overcome old patterns of behavior—or at least not become trapped in them.

The challenge at this stage is to allow myself to be objectified without requiring that the other person who is there help deny my genuine self in the process (a subtle and far-reaching point in terms of "therapy" and "help").

But the liberation is not complete (and sometimes "awareness" seems to make no difference at all, as self-deception reveals motives ever deeper than awareness that are fully capable of using "awareness" for their own purposes).

Therapy at the stage of knowing the frightened child through objectification of the self is limited. It does not deal with the question as to how or in relation to what criterion of value or purpose I should make the new choices. Hence people frequently use therapy to liberate themselves from a painful childhood, only to enter an adulthood based on nothing other than self-assertion. And therapy does not address the experiences of emptiness or lostness that inevitably follow from the projection and objectification of what I had been before. These oversights are accounted for by a simple and naive assumption that seems necessary in order to maintain focus on the freshly identified frightened child aspect of self: that there is a single, knowable set of wants/needs/desires within me, and that if I would just find these then I would be able to live according to them, in harmony with both myself and the universe. But "self" in this understanding turns out to be illusive, endlessly receding over ever-expanding horizons of feeling. Here is what some speak of under the heading of "morbid introspection" or "the infinite regress of motive" as a typical difficulty of the twentieth century.

Failure of this assumption can lead to a typical anger of our era, and enmity—even rage. For this failure (and the discovery that we are not like other animals who appear to have a simple genetic guidance system that moves them gracefully through life) brings us to the abyss, the void, to Nothingness.

Nihilism, as mentioned in the previous chapter, can be defined as arrested development at the edge of the abyss. This includes forms that are expressed as disappointed acceptance of Nietzsche's "will to power" as most basic to life, and to living a life of manipulation, deceit, envy, hysteria, and destruction of anything that claims higher or deeper reality. Again, Nietzsche's statement, "Mankind would rather will the void than be void of will."[89]

It seems especially important to understand this stage since much of "the Psychological Worldview" discussed in the previous chapter is oriented to the manipulative war of all against all "self psychology"; and because, perhaps especially at this moment in history, psychology is so fundamental to our cultural environment.

If I am able to avoid temptations to arrest, and grow beyond nihilism, another quantum leap of consciousness occurs. I discover the other party to the inner dialogue "between me and myself" that has been going on since I emerged from childhood. Who has been doing all this searching? Who has endured transitions from one self-concept to another? Who has been projecting and objectifying? Who is finally brought to Nothingness?

Could it be that failure to confront these questions results in absence of soul? Is this not what Ira Progoff means when he speaks of the need to achieve "a soul beyond psychology"? (See previous chapter).

We come to discover that the sense of sadness and emptiness we find toward the end of the psychological phase is actually an experience of our own vitality and authentic selfhood. The Zen philosopher, Keiji Nishitani makes this point in a helpful way:

> Emptiness is something we are aware of as an absolute near side. It opens up more to the near side than we, in our ordinary consciousness, take our own self to be. It opens up, so to speak, still closer to us than what we ordinarily think of as ourselves. In other words, by turning from what we ordinarily call 'self' to the field of sunyata [Emptiness, Nothingness], we become truly ourselves.... We take leave of the essential self-attachment that lurks in the essence of self-consciousness and by virtue of which we get caught in our own grasp in trying to grasp ourselves.[90]

To make the same point in more Socratic terms, we can observe that "Know Thyself" is initially associated with knowing the frightened self, but in later stages of development it comes to be connected with the riddle of Socrates' potentially confusing confession that he "knows nothing" (as in the Nothingness of nihilism?), or that he hears a "prophetic voice" within (see quote at the beginning of the chapter).

As we move to this riddle and what Nishitani calls the field of *sunyata* (above), we begin to develop relationship with true self, with self that is beyond objectification, and we embark on the journey of spiritualization. Coming to the state that many people today refer to as "living consciously" is not easy. For coming to consciousness requires passage across a fundamental developmental threshold.

INTELLECTUAL FORMATION

Before turning to spiritual development, we need to attend to the intellectual phase.

Intellectual formation may occur, as is perhaps ideal, right alongside psychological development, or before—as with many men in the past, or after—as with many women in the past. In any case there is a profound sense in which the psychological and intellectual constitute two aspects of our humanity that need to be stabilized and harmonized as a prerequisite for the higher order development (as opposed, for example, to the intellect being totally at the service of the psychological—as in Chapter 4). But many mistakes can be made in universalizing and legislating this observation, or in correlating the "two sides" with women and men, right brain and left, East and West, or other easy dichotomies.

With this caution against the temptation of distracting correlation, I will do my best to describe human growth in the intellectual stage along with its benefits and liabilities.

Development of the intellect is necessary for three very central human functions. The first function is to remember what we have experienced in such a way that we can override or transcend conditioning and habit. In this way the intellect enables us to identify and avoid or solve problems. The second function is to organize our experience into knowledge or patterns of meaning about life overall. This makes possible commitment and self-discipline, and a reason to stay focused on a task way past the time when distraction would otherwise intervene. The third function of the intellect is to make it possible for us to converse, and hence enter the kind of relationship in which spiritualization can occur. Through intellect we are able to listen to the statements of others and articulate our own positions on matters having to do with meaning, thereby being able to use the intellect as both a path and a vehicle that allows us, in the words of Plato, to "arrive at the limit of the intelligible."[91]

The mentioning of these general functions of the intellect brings to light the fact that there is a broad range of "applications" of the intellect, and that it can be employed in the service of good or bad moral purposes. The intellect is in this respect very similar to the human hand: it is capable of reaching out and grasping material, working that material into the shape of some plan or purpose, and then employing the object fashioned in the world. Except with the intellect, the material is not physical but ideational, a fact we have been reminded of as our economy has made a transition from physical goods to service and information as the primary resources.

The intellect is one of the most powerful expressions of human potential and of life on Earth generally. In the dominant Western culture of the past, intellect has been the most prized of all human possibilities, and it has been honed and refined to an amazing degree over the past two millennia. Who knows how different life on this planet might be if the human race had identified and honed other possibilities, for example, those represented by mysticism or psychical research. One wonders what line of potentiality was followed by lost civilizations of the past, such as those of Atlantis, ancient Egypt, and the Anasazi Indians, and why (or even if) they are no longer with us.

Now that Western culture is on the verge of being overrun and lost, we see what many of our ancestors failed to see: that the intellect cannot be a complete way of being in itself, that it must act in the service of a higher human capacity if it is to remain healthy. In fact, we have learned that the intellect inevitably will serve values other than its own, that "knowledge for its own sake" and "objective knowledge" were myths—perhaps necessary myths in the phase of human history characterized by movement from superstition and tradition to rationalization.

Presently the intellect serves primarily in the nexus of interaction between the following values: profit, self- interested individualism, technological development, abstract theories of self-help, and entertainment. With our rather recent discovery that the Earth is finite, and that interdependence requires human growth beyond intellectualism (as well as childish and irrational reactions against the intellect), we struggle to redirect the intellect to the service of compassion and caring relationships, the immediacy of vivid experience, and ecological enhancement.

But this is difficult because of the previous faith in the sufficiency of the intellect, whether in the form of faith in correct belief, or in the form of faith in science. The difficulty is the famous twentieth-century crisis of meaninglessness, the discovery of the absurd—the very nihilism we have discussed previously in relation to psychology.

In the midst of the struggle, its strenuousness and ambiguities, we need to be especially alert to that defensive reaction of the intellect called" ideology." With ideology people withdraw from the dialogue of healthy human life between experience and interpretation into a rigid intellectual formulation, a sort of doctrine or dogma. Adolf Hitler and the ideology of the Third Reich is the most obvious example, though cult phenomena and some variants of what I have described as the psychological worldview come to mind once we start thinking about this reaction. It is a typical difficulty within Western culture that has been noticed for some time: Some have seen it beginning with Aristotle and his concern with "first principles" and nothing higher (unlike Plato who, as I mentioned earlier, saw the intellect as a path and a vehicle but not the destination), followed by deduction and verification or application. Intellectualism, as another name for this difficulty, is seen as intensifying at the beginning of the Modern Period with Descartes, and his rigid separation of mathematical mind (excluding anything like "spirit") from the less significant and therefore exploitable body of everything else. By the early twentieth century some, like T. S. Eliot, are concerned about a systematic degradation and loss in Western culture, a drawing back from real life into a pseudo-life of mere information:

> Where is the life we have lost in living?
> Where is the wisdom we have lost in knowledge?
> Where is the knowledge we have lost in information?[92]

I am suggesting that healthy intellectual development moves through precisely this progression from information, to knowledge, to wisdom, to the living of a life. At this point in history it seems that our challenge is to ask the intellect to raise its focus from the level of mere information. This can only happen if we stop identifying with the intellect, if we dare to grow beyond it—not around or under—so as to integrate within our beings a larger embrace of life tensions, possibilities, and capacities.

Both psychological and intellectual stages open onto genuine selfhood and a way of living that is beyond objectification. They open onto spiritualization. But in either case, the opening must pass through nihilism and the dark night of Nothingness. This is what Karl Jaspers was speaking of when he said: "... if man is not to be allowed to founder in the mere persistence of life, it may seem essential that in his consciousness he shall be confronted with Nothingness; he must recall his origin."[93]

SPIRITUALIZATION

Spiritualization begins after cracking the eggshell of projection-objectification and occurs as an opening in which nonobject, genuine self is experienced. It begins with the surviving of *aporia* (see the report on the basic experience with which this book began), knowing nothing as it occurs through interpersonal relationship and life's ordinary letdowns, the experience of Nothingness that is not negative.

Though spiritualization seems to be a natural quality of the life process, it does help to have some guidance. This nurturing of spiritualization includes discipline and direction to guard against movement in strange or dangerous directions, possibilities that are ever-present in the midst of high potential.

One of the greatest discoveries—or REdiscoveries—of our era is of a fundamental human capacity that seems to have been known and honored by all human cultures in the Traditional Period. It has been called "meditation," "mysticism," "contemplation," "contemplative prayer," "sitting," etc. In posttraditional, secular-scientific terms this capacity has been rediscovered as "the relaxation response," or sometimes "stress release," or "peak experience," or even "the flow experience." In our time more and more people refer to it as "mindfulness meditation."[94]

It is an odd historical fact that this discipline of human presence seems to have dropped out of Western culture early in the Modern Period (just about the time of the Protestant Reformation!). In the several-hundred-year period between that time and our own, in stark distinction from other human beings across time and space on this planet, Western people were for the most part deprived of this fundamental discipline. And modernization, the movement out of traditional lifeways and into the way of consumerism that was spawned by the ensuing Western restlessness, carries with it the same alienation from meditation. One is led to wonder about that original alienation and restlessness, how it arose and why it came to have such enormous consequences, and what this might mean in the larger drama of human history.

The drama continues in our time with a return of meditation. It is as though we have discovered that the restlessness of modern activity does not represent the fullness of human potential, but only assertion of ego. We have come to see that the modern individuality may be necessary in order for us to break out of the thrall of ancient collectivities, but that it becomes shallow and dangerous beyond a certain point. In this sense human history, if it is to continue, seems to be understandable in the simplest terms as a movement through three stages: from old collectivities (some very old, some not so old at all) that suppress the individual, to individuality that cares little for community and relationship—or others in any form except that of use, to a new form of life partially glimpsed in our time where synergy between the collective and the individual is sustained.

Here there emerges within the human race the mutual expectation of mindfulness or conscious living: the ability to stand outside of self, and hence participate in an order of responsibility and choice that is rare among our ancestors. Here is a change so great that some have spoken of it in terms of an evolutionary leap.

* * *

But wait! Any teacher would observe that with these remarks I slip from spiritualization into the historical dimension, I digress from the immediate subject of meditation. Along the way in the spiritualization process there are many distractions and false paths: intellectualism (as we have perhaps just witnessed), romanticism, expectation, pride, discouragement,... The list goes on. What is required is the gentle renunciation of all these considerations and learning to meditate (or pray, or contemplate). This is why some have defined "Zen" as "just sitting" (meditation). All we can do is meditate/pray/contemplate, and realize more and more fully that this activity culminates in and is the source of right action, justice, compassion; it cannot be separated from our ordinary activities and relationships but needs to become simultaneous with them.

* * *

There comes a time when one must stop talking about it, or admiring it in others through the work of Carl Jung, Huston Smith, Joseph Campbell, or other cultural mediators of our time. The time comes to simply do it.

This can be an excruciating moment because of all the false and/or "flaky" teachers with whom we are familiar, and because different forms of meditation are tied to religions entailing obligations of belief and membership. Also, we live in a society of sheer and unremitting busy-ness, a society that gets inside of us somehow so that meditation seems a luxury we cannot (or should not) afford (such that luxury cars or condos seem more affordable).

How does one begin? The question is entirely practical, which is to say that it is necessarily individualized. To say "practical," in the full sense, is also to say "art" rather than science, which is to say a matter in which judgment in the midst of unique particulars is far more decisive than any general rule. So the advice that could be given by the writer of a book to the reader of a book cannot be anything other than preliminary.—Yet this might be an advantage.

Learn to meditate. How? It is astonishingly simple—not to say easy: let the mind go blank, and simply accept without any discrimination or action the flow of emotional content that continually passes across the screen of consciousness. Allow that which we know as self descend beneath the turbulence of ordinary, excited awareness on a busy and dangerous planet into the deeper selfhood that can never be objectified and that is one with the larger creative force. Find and trust a discipline of openness and concentration that supports this development.

And be persistent, not worrying too much about ego assessments of how you are doing, how you ought to be doing, or what experiences you should be possessing. Maybe courage, the virtue of the heart (in French, *coeur*) is the decisive virtue.... So much depends on the creativity and initiative of the individual, whether to risk exploration and development of this basic human capacity or not. (There is plenty of room in the process to see the grace of God at work—or not.) I think it helps to know that many traditional forms of meditation contain the understanding that we all have within us what certain medieval mystics referred to as the *magister internus,* a master within us, not unrelated to "conscience," capable of knowing what resources we need and being able to recognize them in their genuine form when they appear. Perhaps this is similar to the Zen saying that may be more familiar: "The master will appear when you are ready." Thus the genuine but initially extraordinary self begins to become the ordinary self.

I have three specific recommendations:

1. Read about meditation. See my recommendation in the last endnote about materials that might be most helpful.

   Perhaps for many people today it would be best to start with the recent scientific evidence about the efficacy of meditation and prayer.[95] —Let us begin with the cathedral within which we find ourselves, that of science! On these terms a very strong case can be made for meditation as a way of coping with the stress any of us accumulates if we move with any vigor in contemporary society. Studies of meditators show very persuasive evidence by all indices: heart rate, galvanic skin response, oxygen consumption, brain wave function, etc.

2. Consult trusted persons near at hand. Be bold to ask religious leaders about their prayer life or meditation practice. Or ask any compassionate and effective person how they maintain themselves in a society structured and driven by technology!

3. Keep in mind traditional and common sense criteria for evaluating things religious. "By their fruits ye shall know them." What are the consequences of the practice? Does it result in my being more compassionate and effective, or not?; more alert and more fully present as my genuine self, or not? Paul Tillich gave a useful list he derived from

> traditional Christian "marks of salvation" (i.e., criteria by which to determine if sanctification was occurring—or something else): "first, increasing awareness; second, increasing freedom; third, increasing relatedness; fourth, increasing transcendence."[96] Henry Nelson Wieman provides another useful list of criteria: "emerging awareness of qualitative meaning derived from other persons through communication; integrating these new meanings with others previously acquired; expanding the richness of quality in the appreciable world by enlarging its meaning; deepening the community among those who participate in this total creative event of intercommunication."[97]

An important general point is contained in most traditional sources on spiritual development: in Christian terms, one's whole life should become a prayer; in Zen terms, it is that we can meditate when cleaning toilets or otherwise going about our most mundane business in the world. In other words, the end of meditating is to stop meditating as an activity separate from the ordinary living of a life, and to progress to the point that one is able to meditate while going about business as usual.

This last, most important point, is beautifully captured in a traditional Zen saying:

> Easy to meditate in the monastery;
> more difficult in the home;
> most difficult in the world.

If the prayer or meditation practice is healthy, it overflows its boundaries and infuses one's whole life. The mark of mature spirituality is not leaving the world, but returning. And further, the returning is not to the world in general, but, more specifically, to compassionate service to others. "The world," which is enormously complex and diverse, is specified as relationship with neighbor such that the high religious figure is not the mystic on a mountaintop but the humble servant to others—as in the Bodhisattva of Buddhism and Jesus as the Christ.

HISTORICAL DIMENSION

We all fall back into our ego from time to time, our "lower self" or, as Socrates said, "the frightened child within."

(Human life is like sailing in unstable air, where sometimes sails will be full with a steady breeze, but other times they fall in on themselves, unhappily becalmed, limp; or sails will sometimes flap with air swirling from no consistent direction, or from tumbling downdrafts. All of these must be accepted somehow.)

But when we human beings are at our best, we are creatures made "in God's image," as creators, as cocreators in the ongoing drama of creativity. We are beings through whom can flow the ultimate energy of ongoing creation, beings capable of direct participation in the action of perfecting (or destroying) this planet. We are openings in the universe through which novelty can flow, the new, that which is surprising, delightful, and redemptive.

This is more than meditation; and the historical dimension testifies to the fact that Earth is more than a dumping ground for Karma. And it is more than the compassionate service that helps others in the work of purifying the soul so as to leave the planet. Human beings are capable of more than purification and leaving. Hannah Arendt is eloquent on this point:

> With the creation of man, the principle of beginning came into the world itself, which, of course, is only another way of saying that the principle of freedom was created when man was created but not before.
>
> It is in the nature of beginning that something new is started which cannot be expected from whatever may have happened before. The character of startling unexpectedness is inherent in all beginnings and in all origins. Thus, the origin of life from inorganic matter is an infinite improbability of inorganic processes, as is the coming into being of the earth viewed from the standpoint of processes in the universe, or the evolution of human out of animal life. The new always happens against the overwhelming odds of statistical laws and their probability, which for all practical, everyday purposes amounts to certainty; the new therefore always appears in the guise of

> a miracle. The fact that man is capable of action means that the unexpected can be expected from him, that he is able to perform what is infinitely improbable. And this again is possible only because each man is unique, so that with each birth something uniquely new comes into the world.[98]

* * *

Though humans have certainly participated in the historical dimension in the past, our times seem to require that many more of us do so, and that our participation be in the mode of stewardship rather than conquest. We must all take as our vocation the saving of the planet! This requirement, as well as resources for meeting it, are available to us through the "historical consciousness" of our era.

In particular, we become aware of three basic periods in human history:[99] The first is the Prehistoric, or the primitive and archaic stages. Here humans, as perhaps in individual childhood, were in a state of dreaming innocence in which there was immediate engagement with the pains and pleasures of the moment. Immediacy was the chief characteristic, and the Earth was experienced as enchanted, which is to say it was inhabited with transhumance agencies of terror as well as wonder.

The second period is the Historical or Traditional. It began around 600 B.C. when an incredible thing happened all across the Earth. Human beings withdrew their attention from the immediacy of direct experience and began to focus on a transcendent realm separate from the Earth. Along with this abstraction came interpretation in the form of the traditions and their sense of historical movement placing their group at the center or apex. These interpretations were nearly synonymous with group identities, and formed the basic enclosures within which humans lived, providing direction and order from within and ways of understanding threat from without.

The third period is Posttraditional or what some refer to as the Period of Humankind. It began in late modern times as traditional identities began to break down under the weight of the transcultural contact made possible by commerce and technologies of transportation, and due to the infectious quality of rationalization, consumption, and materialism. With these forces, humans were alienated from their previous abode in tradition, and hence both isolated and forced together in ways that proved to be unhealthy. Meanwhile, there are wildly conflicting claims about how science and social science can replace the outgrown structures of tradition alongside cults and fascist movements, and T. S. Eliot's death "with a whimper."

Perhaps I have said enough to characterize the Posttraditional Period—since this whole book speaks to problems and possibilities of this phase of human development).

However, there are two other things that must be said at this point:

First, the U.S. must find ways to help the rest of the world, recalling Martin Luther King's statement that "Ultimately a great nation is a compassionate nation."[100]

But there are challenges with this. Some would give the U.S. away, flinging the door open so broadly and getting out of the way to the extent that the U.S. is overrun by the rest of the world, perhaps not in a way that could be described so much in terms of ethnicity or cultural diversity as—ironically—in terms of unqualified capitalism. Others would attempt to close the gates and adopt protectionist strategies and strategies of defensive "help" that would only cause anger from within and without.

Neither of the obvious options work. The U.S. must remain a unity in diversity—neither a free-for-all nor a bastion of privilege. And we have much to learn from the rest of the world, as exemplified in a statement from the Chinese philosopher Tu Weiming:

> Since human rights are understood in a variety of ways according to culture, history, stage of economic development, and concrete political situation, they cannot be universally appreciated as values and aspirations for the global community. Indeed, this accords with the underlying assumptions of Confucian "core values": the perception of the person as a center of relationships rather than merely a system of adversarial relationships, and the belief that human beings are duty-bound to respect their family, society, and nation. These values are not only compatible with the implementations of human rights; they can, in fact, enhance the universal appeal of human rights. The potential contribution of in-depth discussion on Asian values to a sophisticated cultural appreciation of the human rights discourse is great.[101]

One way the U.S. can help the rest of the world—a way that is richly parallel to the Chinese way suggested by Tu Weiming—is through the amazing vitality of its philanthropic groups and voluntary associations.[102] These relational societies, along with educational reform under the heading of "service learning," may be our best hope.[103]

Second, we together in the human race must decide to choose life rather than death, as in the Hebrew scripture:

> I call heaven and earth to witness against you this day, that I have
> Set before you life and death, blessing and curse; therefore choose
> Life, that you and your descendants may live.
>
> *Deuteronomy 30:19*

For us to choose life in our time we must end the threat of that totally negative sense of "Nothingness" that has hung over us since August 6, 1945, like a horrible smog, and which continues to this day in the shape of nuclear weapons: aimed at us and our neighbors as instruments of instant annihilation, oblivion. To not become aware of and take action on this utterly obvious issue is to perhaps exemplify most fully that unconscious nihilism I have cautioned against throughout this work. We must wake up and decide to be cocreators, doing our part to live fully the gift of life that is given.

CHAPTER CONCLUSION

What the Posttraditional Period means for us in our individual maturity, and what the Historical Dimension means as a "highest" phase of human development is well indicated at this moment of our inquiry by two great voices of the twentieth century: Etty Hillesum and William James.

Etty Hillesum is a Dutch Jew who helped many people escape the clutches of Nazism. She reflected on the horrors of her circumstances with the greatest human courage and creativity, and was herself executed at Auschwitz. She spoke of God needing human help:

> But one thing is becoming increasingly clear to me: that You cannot help us, that we must help You to help ourselves. And that is all we can manage these days and also all that really matters: that we safeguard that little piece of You, God, in ourselves. And perhaps in others as well. Alas, there doesn't seem to be much You Yourself can do about our circumstances, about our lives. Neither do I hold You responsible. You cannot help us but we must help You and defend Your dwelling place inside us to the last.[104]

The thought of "helping God" requires us to reevaluate images of God as all-powerful, and "above" any relationship of mutuality and reciprocity.

William James spoke from the very dawn of the twentieth century, from the cusp of transition between the Historical and Posttraditional Periods. After a terrible time of personal crisis, which included encounter with the scientific implication that all is determined in life, he finally decided to believe in his own free will: "My first act of free will shall be to believe in free will."[105] He went further with this theme of choosing what to believe and being responsible for one's belief. He went so far as to suggest that there are some entities in the cosmos whose very ability to be present and available on the Earth may be dependent in part at least on the human willingness to believe in their existence and power—like free will, and love, and God.

Returning to Socrates: maturity occurs when you can hear and be responsive to your "inner voice" in wonder, truth, communication, relationship.... (see Socrates' quote at front of this chapter). But notice that with Socrates the voice never tells us what to do, only what not to do. Here is Socrates' way of affirming human freedom right to the very end!

Cult leaders and other dangerous people might counsel us to follow the voice within that dictates particular thoughts and acts, a voice that so easily becomes eclipsed by neurosis or who knows what! Not Socrates! With him the inner voice, what later Western people called "conscience" (and "law" in a democratic society), does not prescribe specific action. Rather, inner voice maintains to the very end the boundary of that fundamentally open space in which freedom occurs; it will not be objectified!

I conclude with Plato's prophetic observation: democracy in the world, and democracy in the soul have the same form and source—and each both requires and creates the other.

CHAPTER FIVE

DIALOGUE QUESTIONS

1. When you look back over your own life journey, how do you chart your growth as a human being?

2. How is your "chart" related to the developmental pattern discussed in this chapter?

CHAPTER SIX

SOMEONE'S PHILOSOPHICAL JOURNAL

That mood, an expansiveness tinged
  with definite aching,
  melancholia, even mourning, pathos. After what may be
  several incarnations, I finally learn
  this is my genuineness.
It is my source, the place in me both most me
  and where I open onto the energy of creation—being created
  in God's image, as creator: where I myself stand in the draft
  of Being.

In a healthy culture I would be taught
  how to honor this mood, this strange experience from depth.
I would be offered interpretation, discipline,
  authority, companionship in this, in order to let
the extraordinary become the ordinary—in order to become
  myself.

Without cultivation, that this mood might be felt as joy or
  wonder,
I am terrified by the experience (and perhaps terrifying);
I run from it, avoid being alone, mislabel it depression or
  who knows what, or otherwise numb myself
  from intensity within or without.

Philosophy is the thought with which or as which I am active as my own self. It is not to be regarded as the objective validity of any sort of knowledge, but as the consciousness of being in the world.[106]

Karl Jaspers

Knowing ignorance is strength.
Ignoring knowledge is sickness.[107]

Tao Te Ching
Number Seventy-One

INTRODUCTION

We live in a time of extreme contrast that has been well described by Martin Luther King: "...we suffer from a poverty of the spirit which stands in glaring contrast to our scientific and technological abundance. The richer we have become materially, the poorer we have become morally and spiritually."[108]

Our very souls seem to be at peril in a society that drives us to alternate between work that is compulsive and never-ending, and play in which we merely numb ourselves or "chill out." We become alienated from both the satisfaction of creativity and the wonder of recreation (re-creation).

We will be lost in this confusing environment unless we consciously act on behalf of humanity in ourselves and others. And this requires that we be responsible for our basic functions: eating, resting, thinking, our commitments and relationships, what we expose ourselves to artistically and culturally, etc. We must remain conscious, awake, able to choose and act. In Karl Jaspers' terms, we must attend to "the maintenance of selfhood."[109]

I hope this chapter can help readers develop their own hygiene of maintenance and wakefulness. Indeed, the kind of conscious responsibility I am talking about is necessary to effective living in our time of opportunity and danger. And the development of consciousness is the business of philosophy.

In this chapter I share my own philosophical journal, as an example of how one might use writing to support an examined life in a busy world. For me, this has the advantage of requiring a little critical attention to what I have been doing for many years in my own practice of philosophy through journal writing: as an aid in remembering and embodying possibilities that are important to me. Writing has been helpful, in the language of Jaspers' marvelous definition of philosophy above, to remain "active as my own self."

Philosophy takes, as Jaspers says, "the thought," but it also takes knowing how to hold and use the thought in relation to the drama of becoming "my own self." Philosophy turns on Jaspers' crucial phrase: the "with which or as which," or a healthy relation between thought and action—within what Socrates called a life worth living.

Let me elaborate just a moment on Jaspers' utterly basic point: Philosophy is about reminding us (and others, including community) who we are when we are really ourselves. For it seems essential to the human condition that we both experience a genuine, mature, or ideal self, and also experience our alienation or falling away—and hence the need for reminding or re-calling, literally re-membering, within the most general human purpose of becoming who we really are.

But this is a very delicate matter. Because my self is a self and not an object, I must relate to myself. I cannot merely make myself like I make an object, implementing a thought-plan that is separate from the material on which it is applied. Ego "making" itself in a way that drives out soul is the major limitation and liability of the American ideal of the "self-made person": we cannot become our genuine self without the fully human relationship—with self as well as with others.

So my effective reminders to myself cannot be as simple as only commands, formulas, dogmas, or even principles. Sometimes I need to remind by saying *"There":* pointing to this moment, this relationship, this event in which I was fully present as myself, without being able to say exactly what the formula for this presence might be. In order for true philosophy to be effective, it must be a relational art, beginning with that relationship with self out of which "examined life" becomes possible. And it must be concrete, honoring the embodied actuality and mystery of real life. This, again, is not to dishonor interpretation and principle, but only to insist that this function of human life, one that was so highly valued and overvalued in the Traditional Period, be faithful to the fullness of real life on this planet—and in this body.

What follows then is simply my own philosophical journal as it happened one summer.

Of course, it is a little skewed by the fact that I am aware of your looking over my shoulder in your act of reading. This results in not just "self-consciousness," but in an attempt to do more than share my journal "as an example"; I also want to present what I take to be resources, relationships, and insights that can be significant for others in engaging philosophy. But I vow to make every effort to let it be as natural as possible, and to be faithful to Jaspers' definition, one I take to be the voice of Socrates in our time.

However, you will notice as you read along that I have taken out some parts that are just too *private*, not necessarily the same as "personal" or of genuine self. If the material I have now decided to cover over were to be published and appear in public, it would inevitably become something other than what it is, something not intended. It would hurt others, because it is unstable material. It is my primal chaos, my nothingness out of which I struggle with others to create something: a decent world, and a world in which I myself am able to be present.[110]

Also I will confess that the writing component of my philosophical practice in recent years has taken a verse form following my son, Matthew's advice that I develop a more compact way of writing. I have published two books in the verse genre: *Abiding: Landscape of the Soul,*[111] in dialogue with the photography of David Lubbers, and more recently, *Wandering: Brush and Pen in Philosophical Reflection* in collaboration with the Chinese calligraphy of Peimin Ni.[112] Yet I have no other genre name for the short pieces I have come to write. Can I call it philosophy? My colleague and collaborator, Peimin Ni, refers to the writing in question as "philosophical verse." In any event, much of this material first appeared in my philosophical journal.

The verse form is responsive to the concern with interpretation that is so characteristic of our era, the concern to understand that "objectivity" is far more complex than our ancestors had thought and far less removed from the immediacy of lived life. The discovery that Western ancestors engaged the interpretive function too abstractly has led to many movements that want to dive into experience: Existentialism, Pragmatism, Feminism, Philosophy of Ecology, Eastern Philosophy, Phenomenology—all these share a common commitment to affirm and remain faithful to the living, pulsing, struggling reality of lived life. These movements also tend to share the critique of predominant traditional Western forms of interpretation as logocentric, or "intellectualist" in William James' terms, obsessed with what Jaspers calls "objective validity," and being in possession of the first or "highest" principles that allow one to live a life of deduction, dictation, and superiority. Sessila Bok describes this tendency in terms of the assumption of the priority of epistemology, or the need to get things settled intellectually before one can then proceed with a life that is one of application, hence becoming disconnected from real life by refusing to come out from behind abstracted systems of thought.[113] Against this traditional tendency, we also have the problems of contemporary orientations and people who have in effect amputated the interpretive function altogether in the effort to "flow" or "do nothing." "Proteaness" has become a recognizable disorder in our time, as the premature claim to have gone "beyond philosophy"—or, in Buddhist terms, the attempt to "burn the scrolls" before one has mastered them.[114]

My "Philosophical Verse," some more like poetry, others more like journal entries, have helped me be effective with the interpretive function within an examined life. As such, writing in this way helps me think through and remember what is learned in the Socratic "examining both myself and others." It helps remind me of what is important. It allows my finer, more sublime or awake moments to address and guide those moments when I am more numb or asleep, and those aspects of myself that want to follow logics that are at odds with the logic of my genuine self. It helps me stay and become more "active as my own real self," more fully awake or conscious. Or, in the words of the *Tao Te Ching,* itself a verse document, my verse writing helps me avoid the pitfall of "ignoring knowledge"—again, not some abstract, theoretical knowledge, but knowledge in Jaspers' more immediate and modest sense of "the thought with which or as which I am active as my own self."

So I share these writings for what they may be worth in terms of insight—for any sense that they might do for you what they do for me. But they can also be an example of what anyone could do, as a way of giving Jaspers-type messages to one's self. The worth of this kind of writing is also well indicated in the "personal essay" that Laura Duhan Kaplan, for example, practices in her *Family Pictures: A Philosopher Explores the Familiar.*[115] Here, philosophy is grounded, situated, embedded, speaking both from and to where we really live.

So, enough introductions and asides. Here comes my "philosophical journal" from one recent summer.

JUNE 22

> Sometimes it all gets so tight,
> spirit couldn't possibly blow through.
> Like rootbound.
> Here is where the problem is so bad
> I forget I have it.
> Hopefully a friend comes along, or some
> fortunate circumstance (often surprising),
> and wakes me up, opens me,
> moves me to where the breeze is fresh and
> cleansing.

Sometimes it all gets so tight.... Here is a major problem, especially in an era of mechanism: Life gets so busy, there is no open space. None. Each and every moment is "filled" with task and obligation. This is the machine-like quality of life I tried to describe in Chapter 4. It defines "stress."

"The maintenance of selfhood," in Karl Jaspers' phrasing, becomes a major life-agenda. By "agenda" I mean to keep in mind that insidious part of our problem where we are lulled into forgetting we have a problem (recalling Bruce Wilshire's poignant remark about students today: "Missing is any sense that anything is missing").

To maintain myself as myself, I must meditate as a regular hygiene—whether I "feel like it" or not.

But meditation cannot be my entire maintenance. Or, to put

it another way, I must hold to the broadest possible definition of meditation: I must act as though *every* action is an action of self maintenance and meditation. In the midst of the singularity of meditation and the plurality of "every action," I must also keep in mind the following (stated here as simply as possible so as to see the interdependence of these points):

- Be aware of and faithful to those times, events, spaces, activities, and relationships in which I find myself alive, alert, fully awake and present; also be aware of when and where and under what circumstances love, beauty, goodness, and justice occur.
- Be aware in the *practical* sense of taking action, so as to give those moments and circumstances priority within an "examined life." *Talk* with someone about these things. *Do* philosophy!
- Dare to be happy, fulfilled, successful—accepting of the gift quality of life. Dare to live life "to the glory of God." Be alert! Follow the light!
- Keep in mind humble service to others as the best thing I can do for myself.

JUNE 23

I am thinking about what was said yesterday, and specifically the effectiveness of what was said in terms of thought "with which or as which" I can be present as my genuine self. What I said yesterday was cumbersome. It occurs to me today that Martin Luther King says eloquently what I want to say:

> From time immemorial men have lived by the principle that "self-preservation is the first law of life." But this is a false assumption. I would say that other-preservation is the first law of life. It is the first law of life precisely because we cannot preserve self without being concerned about preserving other

> selves. The universe is so structured that things go awry if men are not diligent in their cultivation of the other-regarding dimension.... We are in the fortunate position of having our deepest sense of morality coalesce with our self-interests.[116]

Maintenance of my selfhood is a matter of allowing myself to participate in the first law of life. Philosophy is more about place, space, locating myself in certain relationships—than it is about precise intellectual formulation (which can distract as well as point to where it is we need to be).

JUNE 24

Jesus said, "forgive them, for they know not what they do" (Luke 23:34). What did he mean by this? I offer a contemporary interpretation:

If you don't "know yourself" in the Socratic sense, then you are at the mercy of ego functioning: The ego will assume that it knows everything and is blameless. It will project all limitation and distortion onto others, effectively using them, becoming judgmental, critical, acute in the identification of other peoples' problems; at worst the ego will seek out and prey on the limitations and pain of others, feeding on them. Until we have broken this "old law" (in Christian terms) through death of the ego, we cannot know our psyche and its limitations, the particular ways that we thwart love, justice, real relationship, even our own happiness. Neither can we know our deeper, genuine self that is eclipsed by the hegemony of ego. We can know ourselves in neither negative nor positive senses...we know not what we do.

If you do not know yourself in this way, you literally don't know what you are doing. You will hurt people you do not intend to hurt, you will disappoint yourself—adding fuel to the fire, and you will experience repeated and ever more painful failure. If you don't know yourself in this way, you don't even know how to ask for forgiveness.

JUNE 25

Everything flies by so fast,
we pay attention to nothing,
we pay attention to everything
also, but as if it was on TV
(which it is; though you have to flip a lot of channels.)
And the TV blurs into the mall
and the workspace
where speed is everything
and machines rule.
All humans can hope for is fun.

Everyone, if they feel at all,
feels burdened:
they feel suppressed and muffled,
thwarted in their humanness.
"alienated" was the old European term,
but it has morphed in America:
everyone feels the victim, and
in the perversity of this culture,
we compete for everything, including
victim-rights.

I see that my reading of the current cultural situation is mostly cautionary. Yet here I sit, in the midst of a life so gifted, so privileged. (One maddening quality of our times is that if you say any one thing, then the reverse is simultaneously true as well. This, of course, makes it hard to say anything beyond numbers!)

Being responsible for my attitude, keeping toward the light, is to a large degree a matter of my choice and action. I must act so as to maintain right thinking in Buddhist terms, or exercise "the will to believe" in James', or choose to repeat the more optimistic view of life to himself "as though it were an incantation" in Socrates'. I must heed the American rule of positive thinking! I must quite specifically stick to those thoughts "with which or as which."

So I resist being depressed by my work, and by the world in general—with the overwhelming evidence (as it can always be seen) on the side of cynicism, negativity, etc. I chose this day to adopt the hygiene of healthy attitude!! I accept "depression" as an occupational hazard, and see clearly for a moment the sense in which just living in these times both elevates and depresses.

JUNE 28

The *Tao Te Ching* says: "Ignoring knowledge is sickness." I have a suggestion about how we might understand and use this fundamental point:

In the course of life, the basic insights we need in order to live well and grow *are given*. These insights might come through the remark of a friend, an especially vivid moment of reflection; or they may come quite mysteriously through what we are exposed to by way of culture. The point is that the curriculum of life, if you will, is structured in such a way that we are offered the knowledge we need in order to become who we need to become.

As the Tao says, our problem is so frequently not that we "know not what we do," but rather that we choose to ignore what we know!

To put it another way: how do I get what I know in my intellect to reach my fingers and toes—my everyday, ordinary actions and relations? The mind is an incredible tool. It can perceive importance, grasp knowing, and hold the knowing in memory. But then we become distracted, or so filled up with so much knowing about so many things that we become confused about which knowing applies when, or we become robots devoid of soul who merely apply and forget to relate. —Many are the ways of ignoring.

In my life I need to be alert to the knowledge that becomes available to me, I need to hold it in such a way that it can make a difference without turning me into a soul-eclipsed object, a mere ego constructed out of self-help technologies.

But how? I suggest the wisdom of Aristotle at the foundation of Western culture, Confucius at the foundation of Eastern culture, and in the "virtue ethics" that becomes of interest again in our era when we have discovered the limitations of systems of rules. Aristotle says that I need to habituate myself to good action. In order for this to happen I must practice good actions consciously (rather than arbitrarily or by coincidence), I need to practice them for their own sake (rather than because of any results they might have in my favor—e.g., be honest because it is right rather than because it might impress someone), and I need to keep practicing over some time, being diligent in my cultivation and aware that repetition is necessary in order for the good habit to form[117]—I must not ignore knowledge.

Yet there is another side. On one side, the side represented by Aristotle and the Tao's caution against "ignoring knowledge," I simply need to make my best, sincere, persistent effort. However, somehow at the same time I also need the Tao's counsel about the strength of knowing ignorance, or Socrates' suggestion that his "human wisdom" arises from knowing that he does not know. On this other side, I need to totally renounce all knowing and be as clear and open as I can possibly be to soul/genuine self/God/silence/Nothingness/inner voice....

There is a developmental aspect to this: after the wise and naive innocence of childhood, it appears that I need to *know* in adulthood—and avoid ignoring knowledge—before I can later move to the knowing ignorance; paradoxically I need to act in order to participate in the wisdom of nonaction. Once again, I need to know before I can participate in the wisdom of knowing nothing—or being, in the words of Henry Nelson Wieman, being open to "the infinitely complex and far-reaching network of telepathic feelers" that radiate out from "the creative event."[118]

This could get confusing, frustrating—these two sides, this balance, this essential paradox of human life. Obviously there is some third factor that is most crucial of all. It could be called Greek *phronesis,* practical wisdom; the grace of God in Christian terms; or *Ren*, human heartedness, in Confucian terms.

Some days it is essential to know; other days it is more important to not know; all days require the third factor.

I'll spare the reader the local details and specifics of what it is I need to remember, when it is that I need to be open, and how I am able to discern the one from the other. And I remind myself and the reader: the necessarily more general considerations of any philosophy are only useful if they illuminate and guide this very practical discerning.

JULY 3

My mother died. Because she belonged to no religious organization, I coordinated the memorial service. She had no "religion," yet she was profoundly "spiritual."

At the service I quoted a book she had given me when I was thirteen, Anne Morrow Lindbergh's *Gift from the Sea.* It was her favorite book, and my most cherished inheritance from her. Here is the passage I read, in memorial to Chris Rowe:

> Our grandmothers, and even—with some scrambling—our mothers, lived in a circle small enough to let them implement in action most of the impulses of their hearts and minds. We were brought up in a tradition that has now become impossible, for we have extended our circle throughout space and time.
>
> For we are, actually, pioneers trying to find a new path through the maze of tradition, convention and dogma. Our efforts are part of the struggle to mature the conception of relationships between men and women—in fact all relationships. In such a light, every advance in understanding has value. Every step, even a tentative one, counts. And though we may seldom come upon a perfect argonauta life cycle, we have all had glimpses of them, even in our own lives for brief periods. And these brief experiences give us insight into what the new relation might be.[119]

I see that these statements echo all of the major themes of the book I have been trying to write.

JULY 5 GLINTS

Sailing toward harbor, still far enough away that I am barely able to recognize any detail on the shore, I notice a shiny object near the pier heads I wish to approach. I get flashes, glints, like what is done artificially with strobe lights. These glints make navigation easy. The next several pieces below are of this sort: they are insights that help me navigate.

- Is it possible for humans to move beyond dominance and submission, hierarchy, and competition? Must one gender be dominant, and the other submissive? Does Yin and Yang or some other law require that one sex be the tyrant sex? Must it forever be boss or be bossed? Is spouse abuse of one sort or another inevitable? How hard the human race struggles to achieve harmony, to move beyond not only patriarchy, hierarchy, and authoritarianism, but also senses of equality that reduce us all to a pathetic sameness. The greatest challenge in this struggle is developmental, and the greatest discipline is the relationship of partnership, equality of difference, cooperation, synergy. Identification of this challenge to move beyond the either-or of hierarchy versus low-level equality, as well as provision of helpful guidance as to how to meet what she calls the challenge of partnership, is the reason why Ashley Montagu has said that Riane Eisler's book *The Chalice and the Blade* is "the most important book since Darwin's *Origin of Species.*"[120]
- Richard Tarnas, in his very influential book, *The Passion of the Western Mind,* says that the most general conclusion to be drawn about the history of the Western mind "is that it has been from start to finish an overwhelmingly masculine phenomenon," and that reintegration of the repressed feminine is the major challenge of the present: "Man is something that must be overcome—and fulfilled, in the embrace of the feminine."[121]

Women in these curious posttraditional or posthistorical times are experiencing their "male side." Men are forced to integrate "the feminine dimension." Some women and men overdo it and reject anything "male." Some men and plenty of gender feminist women too (i.e., those who take feminism to be a matter of gender only, permitting women to act like men acted before—even more so sometimes) join a backlash and become hypermacho. Women of this type sometimes ward off any critique of their actions by crying "backlash." It can be very confusing.

In the great sea change of our era, I venture to suggest that men can be feminists as well as women, when feminism is defined as integration of male and female aspects. However, for men this requires a certain death of the sort Tarnas is talking about when he says "the masculine must undergo a sacrifice, an ego death."[122] At least men do not have to deal with—as women do—the temptation to their male side that is offered by gender feminism (except as the temptation to threat reaction—which, I realize, is a pretty big "except"). Complexity; hard to stay steady and centered in a boat pitching and rocking in a sea of irony, fear, deconstruction, cynicism—a sea of everything and its opposite all at the same time!

OCTOBER 20

Today I am doing a little editing of this chapter. At this place in the text I find material I realize cannot be shared beyond the circle of close friends.

In coming to this decision I have recalled what Hannah Arendt said about the French Revolution:[123] essentially private feelings, like pity and anger, resulted in madness when they appeared in public. It was this failure to honor the distinction between private and public that allowed the rapid devolution of "Liberty, Equality, and Fraternity" into heads rolling in the streets.

The next journal entry is an earlier attempt to think through issues of public and private and "personal," and the need we feel to be more intimate than Socrates and the traditional Western philosophers.

JULY 7

Is the kind of journal writing I engage here a practice of the examined life of Socrates, or is it just someone's private processing? Socrates was never personal in the way we have come to understand in our individualistic era, an era in which, as Robin Morgan said, "the personal is political."[124]

At this moment in my attempt to write a philosophical

journal, I need to recall my own cautions about the limits of the psychological. Certainly "personal" consideration can lead us into a wilderness from which there is no return, a wilderness we might not even recognize as such because of the character of our era.

And yet. The personal is also unavoidable. It is a wilderness we must travel through and not around. Again, I recall Ira Progoff's statement about the need to find "a soul beyond psychology."

I proceed, then, in the same faith as that of Karl Jaspers when he says that the only source of a "new and trustworthy objectivity" is "the fidelity and irreplaceability of personal ties."[125] My reflections in this philosophical journal must lead "beyond psychology" to soul, genuine self, clarity, compassion; they must lead to the kind of personal ties out of which these qualities arise—and in which I can be at home in the personal dimension.

JULY 9

ON THE MAINTENANCE OF OLD VIRTUES

We need to insist on maintenance of old virtues, like honor and respect, promise and commitment. In the language of Martin Buber's enormously important twentieth-century book, *I and Thou,* we need to maintain regard for the other human being (even—or especially—a spouse or partner who can become lost in the closeness of our time more easily than in the distance of the past) as a "thou" rather than an "it."[126] We need to teach old virtues because without them people lead lives of unrestrained egotism devoid of discipline or religion, just bundles of self-assertion. We need old virtues because without them otherness is lost.

But ultimately we need old virtues because they are the path by which human beings grow up to achieve fulfillment in relationships of truth, justice, and compassion. The old virtues are the necessary training ground for the highest, best, and most developed human presence we so need today. They teach us to stay tuned to that relationship of cooperation, partnership, synergy—the relationship that is beyond the dilemma of self-sacrifice versus self-aggrandizement, the relationship I have referred to in my earlier work as "the creating form of association."[127]

Without those old virtues—and along with them, perhaps, religion, too—there is no grounding for service or caring (in either public or private), no solid reason for confessing one's limitations, and no compelling urge to lift one's vision above the immediate and the short-term; without cultivation of virtue, humans sink into egotism.

Yet to maintain the old virtues is very different now than it was in traditional times; the challenges and temptations are different.

We must stick to the old virtues, yet with awareness that we are reinventing and consciously choosing culture under conditions quite different from those of our ancestors. One element of difference is that we must simultaneously learn to take care of self. We must maintain self-esteem, be aware of what I need in order to thrive. We must respond to one of the most difficult riddles or (in Zen language) koans of our era: "love yourself." This is very difficult, it is counterintuitive—at least for some of us. (I always think of this point when flight attendants tell passengers who are parents to put the oxygen masks on themselves before their children—in order to be able to save them.)

The dignity and beauty of continuing to live old virtues were vividly present to me recently when I read Huston Smith's *Why Religion Matters:* "The most important thing I inherited from my parents was faith. Its substance made me, on average, a trusting person, and its content can be stated equally simply: we are in good hands, and in gratitude for that fact we do well to bear one another's burdens."[128]

ANTI-RELATIONALITY

Part of the sexism of our era, a part that is perpetuated by the Psychological Worldview discussed in Chapter 4, is that commitment to children (generally, but especially that of fathers) is immediately reduced to behavior that is "obsessional." Motherhood, fatherhood, parenthood—these all become symptoms! Relationship itself is taken as symptomatic, as against the unexamined norm of isolation that prevails in so much of American society.

TRUTH, COMMUNICATION, RELATIONSHIP

Earlier in this book, we have spoken of Vaclav Havel's distinction between "living in truth" and living the lies of ideology and self-interest. In the inquiry of a seminar last winter, I photocopied the longer Havel quote that appears at the beginning of Chapter 4, along with the following statements from Adrienne Rich, Hannah Arendt, and Jaspers. They are very helpful "thoughts" on how and why (and where) to live in truth.

> We begin out of the void, out of darkness and emptiness. It is part of the cycle understood by the old pagan religions, that materialism denies. Out of death, rebirth; out of nothing, something.
>
> The void is the creatrix, the matrix. It is not mere hollowness and anarchy. But in women it has been identified with lovelessness, barrenness, sterility. We have been urged to fill out "emptiness" with children. We are not supposed to go down into the darkness of the core.
>
> Yet, if we can risk it, the something born of that nothing is the beginning of our truth.[129]
>
> *Adrienne Rich*

> The point is that here for the first time communication is not conceived as "expressing" thoughts and therefore being secondary to thought itself. Truth itself is communicative, it disappears and cannot be conceived outside communication; within the "existential" realm, truth and communication are the same. "Truth is what binds us together." Only in communication—between contemporaries as well as between the living and the dead—does truth reveal itself.[130]
>
> *Hannah Arendt*

> There is no generalizable situation, but only the absolute historicity of those who encounter one another, the intimacy of their contact, the fidelity and irreplaceability of personal ties. Amid the general social dissolution, man is thrust back into dependence upon these most primitive bonds out of which alone a new and trustworthy objectivity can be constructed.[131]
>
> *Karl Jaspers*

Truthfulness, truth as a quality of relationship, "the fidelity and irreplaceability of personal ties," "the something born out of that nothing." Access to this way of being requires the death and rebirth experience, the knowledge that is embraced by knowing nothing, the very maturity we struggle to embody.

> OCTOBER 20
>
> Again, I remove some material from the original manuscript, invoking the crucial distinction between "the private" and "the personal."
>
> It is not that taking this material out is to commit self-censorship. On the contrary, leaving it in would be to censor!

JULY 20

Learning the Laws of Ego Functioning

I keep coming back to the problem of getting beyond egotism.

In a way, all concern we have with our self/personal/private amounts to a struggle to peck out of the egg of egotism.

In this society we are having intense and painful lessons on egotism: how it works and why it is a very bad basis for either personal identity or world politics. The human race has tried patriarchy, hierarchy, aristocracy, democracy, mob rule, bureaucracy/management, and free market as ways of ruling the world. Now we seem to be having our biggest and perhaps final experiment with Western individualism, with isolated persons relating only through negotiations about satisfaction of their interests. Capitalism reigns (recalling what George Soros, the wealthiest person in the world, said: that after the collapse of the Soviet Union, capitalism is the biggest danger in the world at this time).[132] It seems final because egotism will either move beyond itself, through discovering the profound interests of the self that are paradoxically beyond selfishness (as in Martin Luther King's "first law of life"), or it will degrade life on the planet to such a degree that no one will even understand the question.

It is best, then, to accept what we learn by way of understanding the laws of ego functioning:

In simplest terms, egotism is a part of all people, one that must be transformed, penetrated, emptied, or addressed in order for the deeper, genuine self to become present on any sustained basis. Ego is a poor "guidance system" for both self and world. It operates as a reflex action that is common to all humans, according to the following laws:

1. It always knows; it will claim full and complete understanding in every situation.
2. It presents itself as perfect; defending itself against any suggestion to the contrary by deflection, rationalization, counterattack, manipulation, lying, or changing the subject.
3. It externalizes its own imperfection/pain/fear by projecting it onto others, seeing in others the very qualities it is unable to see in itself.
4. Ego struggles in its charade until it finally breaks and dies. It is out of this death—this breaking of the ego eggshell—that genuine self emerges. This process of transformation, from a humanities perspective, is the chief topic of the great traditions: for example, Paul in the New Testament says, "I have been crucified with Christ; it is no longer I who live, but Christ who lives in me…." (Galatians 2:20).

Ego just does these things; they are automatic, unconscious. Ego knows not what it does.

JULY 30

Today I think of the French poet Valéry: "There is nothing left to do but to change the self."[133]

I hereby resolve to do this—to change, to accept growth, to grow. I say this without really knowing exactly what I mean. So I offer some more of those "short pieces" as evidence of my struggle (they are the stuff about which the Socratic conversation needs to consider). Where can I find someone to talk with me about these things?!

Everything I do is pathological,
and everything you do
makes perfectly good sense
if you look at it in the right way.

Ego is an imprinted thing; a programmed,
stamped out thing. It was made before I was
conscious. So I cannot "remember" directly,
but must come to understand my "self" as
it is (and was)
reflected off the world.

To "know thyself" is hard. It is like jumping
apart from your shadow.
Maybe introspection isn't even all that important, so long
as I act from true self. Certainly all analysis
is just more egoism until the separation between "ego"
and True Self occurs.
—Yet it probably cannot happen
without analysis, or the crises the planet
has to offer.

Ego knows—endlessly,
and is usually wrong.
the soul has intuition
which is right.
How can we tell between the two?
Here is the main philosophical question.

God seems to prefer
work in the realm
of the impossible.

AUGUST 2

Having submitted these "philosophical verses," I now need to read them in light of the dialogue of this book. I need to read them through the lens of Jaspers' criterion: how do they involve the thought "as which" or "with which" I am able to be more fully present as "my own real self"? How are they useful?

I see that I have been angry. The verse reveals that the obstruction of this anger has been a hindrance to my being able to be present as myself and for others.

Reflecting on this a bit, I see that there are three dimensions to this anger.

First, I am angry at lies and acts of egotism by others, some malicious, committed by particular persons in particular relationships.

But once I admit this, I immediately see that there is another level or dimension: It is I who have somehow required the anger, and teased it out of relationships by assuming that it must be there, or placing myself in relationships where anger must occur. Not that maliciousness has not been real, too, but my own "social construction of reality"—or self-fulfilling prophecy—has been at work as well.

> More private material deleted here (see notes in text above, October 20). Anger obstructs and causes us to neglect or otherwise be distracted from the very relationships that are essential to our vitality.

Here is where Socrates' "know thyself" becomes pertinent. Once I know these things about myself, I become more able to avoid the automatic ego temptation to always blame other people, to "find" in the external world what I cannot tolerate in myself. I need to stay aware of the ways in which I confound relationship, and pollute with my unfortunate imprinting from a past within me of which I can never—even with the best therapy—be fully conscious, and from which I cannot be entirely free. But I need to remain as conscious as I can, exercising the hygiene of awareness of what obstructs my vision and prevents me from being "clear glass." Somehow I need to both accept my ego death, and turn those qualities of personality that can be so problematic toward their positive side.

But, alas, it is one thing to come to insight about ego self, and another to actually change. Paul, in the Christian New Testament, said it well: "For I do not do what I want, but I do the very thing I hate" (Romans 7:15). Again, being conscious and aware, through whatever philosophical interpretation may be devised, is necessary but by no means sufficient. Philosophy must also be about healthy practices, their identification, support, guidance, motivation....

AUGUST 7

The personal injuries about which we worry so much—Was it my fault?/Was it her fault?: they *never* get "figured out" (I think of Adrienne Rich's definition of lying as denial of complexity).[134] Blaming myself and taking on too much responsibility is just another form of lacking self-respect.[135] Blaming the other requires me to live with toxic anger. Here, again, we have one of those frustrating cases of the copresence of two opposing truths: it is all me and my projection; it is all her and her aggression.

To complexify even further, I realize that there is a third dimension to anger, and that is cultural and historical. I think many, many people in this society feel angry today in the sense of being deeply thwarted in their humanity. In the midst of all the technology and entertainment, we are frustrated at not being able to find community and home and family that is sufficient to who we really are. I think we feel angry about the loss of enchantment, tradition, God.... We are enraged at the pathetic quality of a society of competition and consumption that is thin soup indeed in the nourishing of a human soul: we are all victims! In America, we are victims of our own success, our selfishness, our urge to control.

Considering the three dimensions of anger together, I see that anger is associated with evil—when we understand evil, along with Nel Noddings and other integrative feminists of our era, as that which causes us to "reject the impulse to care."[136] Anger obstructs and results in our neglecting our otherwise being distracted from the relationships that are essential to our vitality.

AUGUST 8

So what resolves my problem and relieves the blockage? What thoughts actually help me live the vitality of my genuine self, as opposed to the seductions of ego, including that of toxic anger?

Well, the very act of speaking helps. The act of confession itself brings relief. And here, I suggest, is one important function of a philosophical journal: it can be useful in the elimination process, it can help us bring to consciousness our distractions and fears so that we might take action, and hence grow toward clarity and compassionate presence.

Note that some social scientists today are "discovering" that forgiveness is good for us, the healthy thing to do.[137] But forgiveness is different from elimination. Forgiveness requires a person, a relationship, action by an other.

In the forgiving relationship, I come to "know" myself in relation to such matters as are contained in my confession, and I also meet the despair and impossibility of my ego self, the limitedness of "self" in any objectifiable sense. Once this self has "died," hard as it is, I then experience, even if only briefly, a very distinctive warmth and expansiveness, a cleanliness or integrity; I experience what I referred to as "an expansiveness tinged with definite aching" in the verse piece at the beginning of the chapter (or in references to *aporia* throughout this book). I experience my genuine self, my vitality, and hence also the possibility of being in the world as a being who is both limited and free. Again, the theme is nothingness and maturity. Stanley Rosen indicates the importance of this in relation to the future of philosophy when he says "if philosophy is to be preserved ...it must come to terms with the Nihil Absolutum."[138]

Also again, the dialectic between knowing and knowing nothing.

Yet this dynamic is not possible in the isolation of my journal (or in "therapy" in which the professional fails to appear as a person), no matter how rich in insight it might be. Forgiveness is not possible in the relationship between me and myself that the practice of journal writing can strengthen and develop, though this practice and cultivation of healthy relationship with self is very important. There remains something absolutely fundamental and irreducible about human relationship: we see it in Jaspers' point about "the fidelity and irreplaceability of personal ties" as the only source of "a new and trustworthy objectivity," in "the new relation" about which Lindbergh speaks, in the Christian understanding that Christ is present "where two or three are gathered in my name" (Matthew 18:20), and in Socrates' insistence that talking with others each day is the very best thing we can do for ourselves.

Journal—or any writing—can only be preparation for encounter.

It should also be said that the very particular kind of relationship to which I point is very rare. But it is also compelling, perhaps necessary for the future of the human race—certainly for the future of American culture, as is indicated by Lindbergh's statement about our needing to be pioneers. Peter Hershock, in *Reinventing the Wheel: A Buddhist Response to the Information Age,* speaks in helpful ways of the kind of relationship we seek as a "truly liberating intimacy:" "...a new kind of intimacy. Pursued in the spirit of expressing a truly liberating character—a character constituted not by the drawing of clear and controlled boundaries, but rather their erasure.... Virtuosity is a trail we blaze only at high risk, by opening ourselves to maximal intimacy and so maximal vulnerability with and before the people and things sharing our narration."[139] I also recommend Ralph Harper's magnificent, short book, *On Presence,* for its practical value in living the essential human relationship. He speaks of "...dying to self and follow[ing] the echo of whatever good presence we may find."[140]

AUGUST 12

Philosophy is unavoidably therapeutic;[141] if it is about anything it is about transformation. In this way it is like (or includes) psychology, though the tragedy of so much "psychology" as a contemporary practice is that it replaced human openness with pseudoscientific closure, not-knowing with knowing, losing faith in the saving power of *aporia* as that moment in a human encounter when possibilities open up and become available to us. Something happens in the fully human relationship that happens nowhere else.

Philosophy needs to be personal in the relational sense, beyond mere privacy and emptying of internal, psychological content. Not to say that there is not importance to this function, but that it must not be mistaken as the only function of either philosophy or psychology. In its larger and complete sense, philosophy (and psychology) move us toward the world, toward "liberating intimacy" and healthy vocation—and protect us against the ever present human danger of collapsing in on ourselves.

"World" means individual relationships, groups, associations, communities—the broad range of our shared life. It also indicates and includes our participation in the historical dimension: the fact that my story is never just my story only. For example, my own particular story in part is testimony to a reality that has been heresy and "politically incorrect" or "inappropriate" up to the present: that there are forms of domination and control, ones that sometimes find it useful to claim the legitimacy of science, therapy, or feminism that have not been acknowledged to this point. These forms of domination and control are associated with a fairly simple and thoroughly pessimistic assumption: that everyone is (or should be) "angry"—that anger is a (or the) basic life-response, and that "expressing" and thereby "letting go of" one's anger is the highest value. Not that there is no truth to the reality of anger in human life and the danger of holding this feeling, but when it becomes *the* truth, to the point where people are instructed to be angry and cultivated in their anger, the war of all against all follows. The key to understanding the worldview of anger is in the meaning of "anger"—which is hard to define. It can be identified at least partially by its overlap with other toxic qualities of our current cultural condition: suspicion, deconstruction, envy, negativity, resentment, and the refusal or inability to sustain effective belief in any realities higher than materialism and self-interest.

...Philosophy needs to speak the unspeakable, and thereby open new possibilities for relationships of mutuality, appreciation, and growth. And this opening, by definition, entails risk, the breaking of taboos, and the effort to say what has not yet been said.

(An apology to the reader: what I have just said in this entry is not fully articulated. I am not yet able to speak fully, indicating work I need to do in the future, as the private becomes personal and then public. Several references in earlier parts of this book describe the same cultural condition to which I point more effectively than I do. I especially recommend Richard Stivers', *The Culture of Cynicism.*[142])

AUGUST 14

Last week my son, his friend, and I drove to Lake Michigan. Upon seeing a hawk wheeling above a woodlot, Kev's friend, Brock, asked: "What's the purpose of birds anyway, what do they do?" I did my best to explain about their eating bugs, etc. But he was following a powerful and much deeper line of questioning, and before I could finish with my explanation about birds and the ecosystem, he moved on to the purpose of other animals, and very quickly came to the question about humans: What is the purpose of human life?

We talked a little and then didn't talk, enjoying the magnificence of that bird against the wide, blue Michigan sky. It occurred to me that our silent enjoyment was a sort of answer to the question, and then I recalled a poem that Huston Smith had cited in *Wandering*:[143]

> Four ducks on a pond,
> A grass bank beyond,
> White clouds on the wing,
> What a little thing
> To remember for years,
> To remember with tears.

The "answer," our human purpose, is in the consciousness of these luminous moments of simple rightness, of eternity in time and space, the union of heaven and earth (in the Confucian understanding of heaven as *tien*, more under than over the earth, certainly not displaced in a separate realm), soaring like the bird—and aware, appreciative, free.

Dialogue with children can be so lucid.

AUGUST 16

I heed William James' suggestion about "the will to believe," his point about some realities depending for their very existence on this planet on the willingness of human beings to sustain the belief in them—recalling also the poignant words of Etty Hillesum, "God needs us,"[144] and Socrates' advice in "Phaedo" that we "risk the belief" in such things as the immortality of the soul as a support to living the sort of life that is worth living. —Or the Christian point about salvation being a free gift, if we would just dare open our hearts and believe; or the Confucian sense of the human (*Ren*): "It is human that can make the Way great, not the Way that can make human great."[145] One basic meaning of the Hebrew notion of humans being created "in God's image" is that we are created *as creators*, and that we create through what we choose to believe.

It is with this advice and in response to Jaspers' suggestion about thoughts "with which or as which" I am able to be myself, that I feel the conclusion to this philosophical journal approaching. I end, then, with telling you (and me) the thought I most need to hold and believe:

I learn to "send energy" to those I love and care for as well as learn to receive energy from them. In the language of Madeleine L'Engle's *A Wrinkle in Time,* which I first read in the context of my daughter, Kristin's religious education, we gradually learn to engage the "tesseract", whereby we can be with and support others across great physical distance (and psychic, too).[146] But perhaps this sounds too strange or "new age." My Chinese colleagues in *qigong* practice are able to project their *qi*;[147] Thich Nhat Hanh, speaking from a card on our refrigerator door, says, "The energy of love is abundant, waiting to be called upon." The efficacy of prayer has been proven by science.[148]

Here, then, is my most important thought: the unnamable source of our vitality flows directly through us, though most of the time at a slow and meandering trickle, since it is obstructed by ego. When we open our hearts and allow it to flow more freely (stop refusing the gift for our egotistical reasons), it benefits ourselves as well as the world into which it flows; and the opening to greater and more pure flow occurs most effectively when we are in compassionate relationship with other human beings.

CHAPTER SIX

DIALOGUE QUESTIONS

1. If you were to keep a journal as a support for an examined life, what sort of commitment would be appropriate for you? —Writing once a week, once every two weeks? I suggest collecting miscellaneous notes, observations, and quotes in a folder and then sitting down periodically with your journal to write about what you have collected and whatever else is significant.
2. When will you read, and where? And what? What are your sources of advice about what, in a world of information overload, is worth reading? What is your discipline or method for reading? Who can you read with?
3. What people or associations are your best sources of dialogue? Given this awareness, how do you wish to shift your priorities in terms of cultivation of friendship?

CHAPTER SEVEN

PHILOSOPHY, DEVELOPMENT, AND THE WORLD

> Democratic pluralism, on the face of it a fine position, cannot be espoused in today's world as if all we had to do was *choose* it. To achieve a truly egalitarian pluralism conceptually and politically, it is necessary for all groups to achieve self-knowledge, developed from within rather than imposed from without.[149]
>
> *Elizabeth Kamarck Minnich*

> We are at a critical juncture to move beyond three prevalent but outmoded exclusive dichotomies: the traditional/modern, the West/the rest, and the local/global.[150]
>
> *Tu Weiming*

It is not adequate to conclude in the realm of the personal, as in the last chapter. If we are faithful to philosophy in the full sense, the *service* aspect must be maintained and cultivated—and honored as the prior dimension of philosophy. Faith in philosophy is manifest as service, a willingness to bear the burden of negative evidence as to the possibility of goodness in the world—and to *take action*. Stated in terms of individual philosophers, this is to say that we always need to "return" to the world, as in Plato's *Republic*, either by our own enlightened choice or by public demand. From the perspective of the larger origin of our philosophical tradition, it is always appropriate for us to insist that philosophers be present in the world!

On this note, I want to conclude *Living Philosophy* with my own most current and compelling engagement in the world. This chapter, then, is an instance of philosophical practice in the public, and advocacy of the role of philosophy in public life. I try my best to live up to the ideal of philosophy as helpful, effective, presence in the world as we actually live it. In this attempt, the chapter that follows also demonstrates the thesis of the book overall: that philosophy as Socratic practice comes alive and available through dialogical contact with the other—in this case, China.

Taking the world seriously raises the issue of progress, development, or movement to maturity in history—in the larger drama of the human race and the planet Earth. Can our commitment to the world make a difference? Clearly Western culture has been embarrassingly naïve and simple-minded about "progress" in the past. But this does not mean that we should or can give up on this dimension, pursuing individual development only. Here is one of the dangers of postmodernist culture and philosophy, with its endless irony in relation to the world, which, whatever else it might signify, amounts to failure of engagement.

My suggestion is that we must choose and maintain a healthy belief in the possibility of positive movement in history, one to which we can lend our talents and our strength. Texts or scripture on this utterly crucial point are by now familiar: Socrates when he says he doesn't know—I don't know that there is *not* progress! Also William James on willing to believe, and his related point, shared also by Etty Hillesum, about there being some energies in the universe that may depend at least in part on our willingness to sustain the belief in them (maybe our belief helps bring them near). Finally, I recall again Socrates' point in "Phaedo" about the necessity of maintaining beliefs as integral to the living of a healthy life. Of course we must be aware of the dangers of naïve optimism, but on the other extreme we need to know that our decision to engage with the world and its improvement can never wait on conclusive evidence. Neither can it be strictly a matter of maintaining my own health. The call of the world and of our common humanity ultimately must be felt religiously, as a response to the deep spiritual message woven among the world's great traditions: that life is a gift, that our actions matter, and that we can be at home on this planet.[151]

I.

In recent years I have been fortunate to participate in what some of us have come to refer to as "the vocation of cultivating mutual understanding and growth" between American and Chinese people. We have realized that this cultivation between people and cultures may be the best hope for the human future. Our work has been guided by a basic vision: of this century as one of growing together in respect and appreciation, as residents of both particular cultures and a single planet—as distinct from the last century, which so largely consisted of conflictual relations between governments. The reality and the urgency of bringing this vision to embodiment was announced dramatically at the beginning of our new millennium, by the events of 9/11/01 and the ensuing struggle with terror.

"Dialogue" has become the operative term for the kind of encounter we seek to convene and cultivate.[152] This term is difficult to articulate because it indicates a developed human capacity that seems to transcend cultural boundaries. There are three aspects to dialogue, which I will state in relation to my own experience with Chinese culture: (1) As a Westerner, I have discovered and benefited very greatly from the riches of Chinese culture and my associations with Chinese people; I have learned and grown. (2) Out of participation in dialogue I have also rediscovered and found new vitality in my own inheritance as well. And (3) through both of these aspects of dialogue there has emerged the third which is hard to state: for now I will just say I have found a way to live more fully and faithfully as a world citizen and a mature human being.

In this chapter I would like to share my reappropriation of Socrates as a powerful resource for living and relating, including as a way of articulating the richness of dialogue with Chinese culture and people—and intercultural dialogue generally. At the same time I will attempt to share the developmental process through which reappropriation and the magic of dialogue occur. Finally, I would like to say a few things about the emergence of dialogue in relation to a new enlightenment period and the healthy formation of world community.

II.

In the kind of reappropriation I am talking about, "dialogue" comes before "Socrates." This is to say that the Socratic approach I have come to is itself a product of dialogue; it is a "rediscovered" Socrates, an appreciation and awareness of Socrates that only emerges out of encounter with the Other. There is a central and unavoidable paradox here, one with which I think Socrates was familiar: it is only through open or mature relationship with the other that I can come into the full appropriation of my own tradition and integrity.

I was not always at this point. Some description of the developmental process through which I/we come into the capacity for dialogue seems utterly crucial in our time. How much the developmental process as I describe it can be generalized or universalized is a big and profoundly important question. We have been very shy about generalizing in postmodernist times, but perhaps the world that follows 9/11 requires us to go beyond the post-modernist relativism; in the terms of Huston Smith, 9/11 requires us to move "beyond the post-modern mind."[153] Perhaps we are ready for a new universalism, a new enlightenment period of humankind. This is certainly something I want to discuss more fully with persons of other traditions.

Importance of clarity about human/cultural maturation in the world that follows 9/11 seems clear. For it seems that we as citizens of the world, must insist, not that anyone give up their religion or tradition, but that everyone come to the cultural and personal (and religious) maturity to be able not only to tolerate other points of view, but also to learn from them (without affirming all of them; certainly not those that are destructive of the new universality of humankind, united in both similarity *and* difference, that is emerging in our time). We must be willing to learn and continue to grow, accepting that our present position is not final, that neither we nor our culture is perfect. This, obviously, is asking a lot of human beings.

Let me state the developmental process as I have experienced it briefly and boldly, as a hypothesis to be tested in further dialogue: Human beings and cultural orientations pass through three basic stages in order to reach maturity in the posttraditional world situation and capacity for dialogue.[154]

1. Absolutism/Traditionalism: Closed culture, vast majority of humans "enveloped" in a shared metaphysic—i.e., basic understandings of life, death, meaning, value, morality, and justice. Here "others" are enemies, less than we, and/or exotic (i.e., projection of our own Jungian "shadow side"). Cultural answers are given, final, beyond question.
2. Relativism: Discovery of the legitimacy of the other and the fact that there might be more than one "right answer." This discovery is usually accompanied by "modernization," influx of consumer values, and social science/psychology in ways that cause the basic discovery to collapse to the lowest level of "will to power" or self-interest or, as we say in America, "Whatever." Dialogue among cultures and people about how to address this shared interim condition in the Posttraditional/Postcolonial world could be effective not only for personal awareness but also for social policy.
3. Dialogue: Out of surviving or rekindled longing for "higher values" and a fully human life, the ability to learn from others, to allow this learning to nurture our own root identities, and a way of living that is "both definite and open."[155]

Returning to the specifics of dialogue with Chinese philosophy and people, I can say that I have learned both deep critique of Western culture (deeper than that of either deconstructionists or neoconservatives from the West). In the process I have been able to appropriate fundamental resources of insight and practical living from China. But what is more, I have also come into contact with the riches of my own tradition in a way I never could have imagined—contact in ways practical as well as just intellectual.

I want to share the story of this movement, beyond traditional absolutistic readings of Socrates—which largely used him as a literary device for the delivery of what had become Platonic doctrine in the West. I will begin with the relativism of the present, characterized by the deconstructionist urge to merely criticize on one extreme, and the simple neoconservative assertion of whatever they call "tradition" as a shield—and potentially a weapon—against the relativistic decadence of the present cultural situation at the other extreme (which in most extreme forms becomes fascism and the fanaticism with which we have become reacquainted recently). From here, the Catch-22 of these two positions—as well as from the relativistic chaos that lies between, I want to speak about movement into the reappropriation I mention, a reappropriation that is paradoxically definite yet at the same time willing to admit mistakes, both past and present, and open to those others with whom the mutual growth of dialogue occurs.

III.

So, the story, beginning in the relativistic stage of Posttraditional, Postabsolutistic Postmodernism:

In the twentieth century, there arises a well-known critique and "deconstruction" of Western philosophy and culture, a radical relativizing. The problem with the Western influence on the rest of the world is understood to be deeper than the Modern/Enlightenment orientation. The problematic modern world of self-interested individualism, unqualified rationalization, and unexamined assumptions of Western superiority is understood as an intensification of what had been going on in Western culture for centuries. Beginning as early as Aristotle, the West had been dominated by obsession with certainty, abstract knowing, and objective proof. Early on there set in a strong urge to distance ourselves from real life into the purity and supposed protection of intellectual "first principles."

With Descartes and the beginning of the Modern Period, the distance intensified further. The mind of first principles came to be separated from the body of lived life, including the Earth itself. The body of self and society devolved into the competition of isolated individuals pursuing their "self-interest," understood in terms of material goods, their acquisition, display, and consumption. Meanwhile, "mind" became ever more mathematical, as the instrument of calculation in relation to "interest" in its narrow definition. From our perspective today it seems obvious as to why the Modern Period in the West would end with themes of alienation, diffuse anxiety, revulsion, and existential revolt.[156]

The dominant philosophical tradition, which both informed and reflected these developments, was finally expressed in the narrowness and abstraction of the analytical and linguistic movements in the late nineteenth and twentieth centuries. Philosophy had lost touch with so many people and so much of the joy and sorrow of real life that even some philosophers began to speak of "the end of philosophy."

The point of this familiar critique of Western philosophy, around which so much of philosophy is active today, is that the dominant forces became overly rational, logocentric, "male," and incoherent in terms of life in the world we share as embodied beings. Philosophy even became dangerous sometimes. Witness, for example, Martin Heidegger's association with the Nazis, or the incoherence of Richard Rorty's "poeticizing."[157]

In the immediate present, philosophy certainly has become "reflexive" or self-critical. But where is the positive direction or vision? Getting beyond the relativistic stage can be seen as an overarching issue and agenda for Western philosophy today.

In my own work of seeking positive direction for philosophy and Western culture (my work of "reconstructing philosophy," in John Dewey's sense), I needed to "leave" Western philosophy for a time, develop a broader multicultural view, and learn in some depth the strengths of other cultures—especially (for me) the culture of China.

Many of my Western colleagues have followed a similar path. For as the twentieth century came to a close, the analytical stronghold in philosophy finally broke up. With release from the thrall of mathematics, notions of cultural superiority, and the need for rigid separation between "philosophy" and "religion," a very exciting, new, Posttraditional Period has begun in the West.

The West—no less isolated than the East historically, though in different ways—opened up to the rest of the world, including the worlds of Eastern philosophy, Feminism, and Ecology.

The West began to move beyond its insistence that there can be only one right answer and that we must claim to have its proper intellectual formulation (and that possession of right doctrine is sufficient claim to superiority).

Initial contact with otherness frequently led to confusion, relativism, cynicism, and a general lowering of human ideals and expectations in the midst of a world of machines and entertainment. But contact also led to identification and appropriation of elements from other traditions that had been lost in our own. Speaking specifically about the dialogue with China, from the best of traditional Chinese culture Westerners are learning how to be at home in what William James and Tu Weiming call the "thick" of existence.[158] We are learning acceptance of what is, and to find repose in and through the depth of the actual. We are learning to appreciate the state of well being *(xing fu)*, to live with sincerity or honesty *(xin)*, becoming both more simple and more complex than we had been before. And we are beginning to learn living with "smoothness" or "throughness" *(tong)*, honoring the gift quality of life. In all of this, we have gained fresh insight into the cultivation of the human being *(xue)* through which these qualities become manifest in ordinary life.

However, we did not simply attempt to become Chinese, though this has been a temptation for some, and a typical way in which dialogue has failed in our era—the attempt to identify with the other. For in the fullness of dialogue there is another crucial element, and that is identification and reappropriation of what is best in one's own tradition, such that contact with otherness has also led to new embodiments of what is truly vital in the West.

IV.

What is this greatness of the West?—this "rediscovered" Socrates?

Briefly stated, there has been a realization that the origin and energy of philosophy lie in a transformative praxis of human encounter through which we are able to drop our illusions and false knowing in such a way as to gain greater access to a more profound knowing and living that comes simultaneously from "the religious dimension" and our own genuine self.

The fullness of Socrates' famous statement in the *Apology* about "the unexamined life" says it all!

> I tell you that to let no day pass without discussing goodness and the other subjects about which you hear me talking and examining both myself and others is really the very best thing that a man [*sic*] can do and that life without this sort of examination is not worth living.[159]

Hence "philosophy" is a way of living, that includes—but is not limited to—ways of thinking, which now can be consciously evaluated and chosen. The vitality of philosophy is more a matter of recovering practice than of arriving at correct intellectual formulation. From the perspective of the rediscovered Socrates, I have suggested that vital philosophy must have three interrelated components of practice, which we can see earlier in the Western philosophy with Socrates: discourse, service, and contemplation or meditation. In the absence of any of these components, characteristic problems develop. In Western history, when service and meditation dropped out, it was more or less inevitable that the discourse element would drift and be distorted in the direction of dangerous displacement into intellectualism.

"Discourse" seems obvious and simple at first, though in any serious engagement with this component we learn the depth and complexity of this inclusive, relational practice. As "the very best thing a man [*sic*] can do," philosophy is relational/associational/communal. This makes "service" absolutely necessary; as the commonly shared effort to change the world for the better, as in Socrates' service to Athens.[160] For, as Plato pointed out, the form of community and the form of self are the same. Philosophy also requires "meditation," or the contemplative aspect, as both preparation for the human encounter/relationship that is central to philosophy, and as integration of the growth that occurs through this practice. Meditation teaches us that knowing of genuine self requires more than intellect; it requires silence as much as words. Meditation, including the full meditation of presence with the other in love and justice, means deep listening, as in the mysterious "standing" of Socrates and his relationship with his "inner voice."[161]

Philosophy as praxis, then, *is* dialogue with others, including my "self" (between the aspect that can be objectified, and the aspect that is beyond any description). Dialogue entails both "know thyself" and also the kind of openness out of which I can truly *hear* the other. At the same time and perhaps more deeply, philosophy as dialogue brings me to the critical state of *aporia*—to the realization that I do not know what I thought I knew, and hence to the "knowing nothing" of Socrates, and through this state to contact with the "inner voice" or "prophetic voice" which "has always been my constant companion, opposing me even in quite trivial things if I was going to take the wrong course."[162]

This way of philosophy –and along with it the Western tradition of liberal education—is not just about information, but transformation. Cultivating the developed human ability to be simultaneously open and definite, to be fully present, this way of philosophy values full human relationship and what has been called democratic community above all else.

As Plato indicated, philosophy transforms both the individual and community, never one at the expense of the other—as was so often the case in the Western history and social/political thought that followed (alternately emphasizing the individual in ways that harm community, and forms of community that violate individuals, rarely the democratic relationship in which both are affirmed simultaneously). The key again is democratic relationship, a fundamental quality of life that is relevant to our selves, God, and nature as well as to our human others—such that we can speak of democratic personality, democratic religion, and democratic ecology as well as democratic community.

V.

With reappropriation of the Socratic approach, we come into participation in what Huston Smith, the great *jnana* yogin philosopher of our time, refers to as Western "philosophy as a world religion."[163] Western philosophy comes into focus as one of the world's great traditions of transformative practice.

As indicated above, in the description of my own journey with Chinese philosophy and the "rediscovered" Socrates, there are several crucial developmental steps beyond relativism through which we enter into participation in "philosophy as a world religion." First, we come to awareness of what Smith and others call "the perennial philosophy,"[164] the realization that at the depths of all of the great traditions human beings share a profound and ineffable commonality. Our limited human languages and cultures each celebrate, articulate, and practice imperfectly in relation to that which is common. We experience an "objectivity" or sense of the Absolute, now from "below" rather than from "above," as in the absolutism of the Traditional Period. This is to draw a subtle and decisive distinction: between traditional human experiences of the Absolute as given through the authority of commandment and/or cultural inheritance, as opposed to the direct personal experience of commonality at the root of diversity in our post-traditional times.

The second stage is one of reappropriation or reengagement of our "own" tradition, a "return" to the particular, limited tradition from which we arise, now appreciated as a doorway to the universality perceived in the first stage. Failure to cross the threshold into this second stage is often expressed in our time as a universalism that is really aesthetic and social instead of religious, an orientation that admires the commonality discovered in the first stage apart from the humbling discipline of practice within any one tradition. This preliminary or false universalism is located ambiguously between the Postmodernist relativism and the authentic univeralism to which we must turn next. The preliminary universalism contains the dangers of aestheticism that have been well observed in the past, from Kierkegaard to students of aestheticism in Nazi Germany and Western Orientalism.

There are dangers, then, to the developmental pathway I seek to describe. In addition to the danger of the aestheticism associated with the first stage just mentioned, there is also a danger associated with the second stage. It is the danger of reactionary or fanatical return. The first stage of apprehending "the perennial philosophy" is delicate and challenging in ways that can be overwhelming or frightening. One response can be a "return" to one's particular tradition that is cynical, founded in resignation, or driven by the simple need for shelter from the ambiguities of living beyond absolute knowledge, certainty, and the wish for submission to unquestioned authority. "Mankind [humankind] come of age" requires a kind of courage and faith that cannot be taken for granted, a kind of support and guidance that is not always present.

If, by whatever grace or good mentoring may be present, we are able to walk the thin line between the dual dangers of aestheticism and fanaticism, then we begin to enter a third stage—of universalism in the fully religious sense. There is an essential paradox here, one I have previously described as the paradox of simultaneous openness and definiteness, and in terms of the realization that what is most profoundly common among human beings is our need for transformative practice. The paradox is that access to this new universality, we might say the doorway to a new enlightenment period that is "beyond the post-modern mind," only comes through the particular—through what Tu Weiming calls "the globalization of local knowledge."[165] The way of genuine or mature universality is not to "transcend" or stand outside of, as in the older, European Enlightenment, but rather to engage in the "thickness" of both our own tradition and dialogue/discourse with others who remain different, even as they become friends—within what Hannah Arendt called "the paradoxical plurality of unique beings."[166] Dialogical contact with others different from myself who are also engaged in transformative practice helps me in various ways: it leads to insight, it motivates, it inspires—and it provides necessary companionship.

Within "philosophy as a world religion" it becomes possible to appreciate, practice, and embody the way of Socrates more fully than before. This *includes* the reflexive capacity to accept criticism and the limitations of Socrates: Where do we see compassion in Socrates, love that heals the egotism at the root of his interlocutors' logical fallacies?; Where do we see Socrates' willingness to submit himself to the same clarifying process he administers to others?; Where do we see guidance in relation to the "mystical" or meditation component that was evidently so important to Socrates himself?

Now, grounded in the definiteness of our Socratic inheritance in the global context as world religion, we become capable of growth, of openness and real learning from other traditions. In the maturity of a new enlightenment we are released from the postmodernist stage, either entangled in endless, deconstructive criticism or locked up in defensive neoconservative assertion. For example, Chinese and Eastern traditions help us understand and develop the meditation component of the Socratic tradition, so we can see and actualize what has been overlooked and underdeveloped in the writings of Plato. With help from Eastern friends, previously obscure passages take on new significance. Consider the following: "Acquaintance with it must come rather after a long period of attendance on instruction in the subject itself and of close companionship, when, suddenly, like a blaze kindled by a leaping spark, it is generated in the soul and at once becomes self-sustaining."[167] Could this be "Enlightenment" in the Eastern sense—or the very movement to maturity we must be concerned with in our time?

VI.

As I suggested at the beginning of this essay, maturation into the developmental stage where dialogue becomes possible is an urgent matter in the post 9/11 world. For me, as a Westerner and an American (who I am!), it seems appropriate to conclude this essay with an attempt to "apply" the perspective I seek to make available, not to Chinese or Afghan cultures—though this is certainly important also—but rather to my own. So I conclude with some reflections on the U.S. situation, a suggestion about how "the Socratic approach" might be helpful. This I do in the companionship of not only Western/American colleagues, but also Confucian and Daoist friends who are doing something quite analogous.

Through the horrendous events of 9/11/01 and following, the U.S. is beginning to gain some perspective on what George Bush Sr. called the "new world order."

Coming to a healthy perspective is challenging because so much of American culture is in the grips of the question: Why do they hate us so much? Response to this underlying question combined with temptations to avoid it through obsession with the very real but illusive enemy, terrorism, constitutes the primary challenge to America in the new millennium.

Addressing the question and moving to a broader perspective on the place of the U.S. in the world community is, above all, a developmental challenge to Americans, the challenge to move to a more mature way of relating in and with the world. It requires recognition of the attitudes of self-righteousness, superiority, and even arrogance the U.S. has taken in the past. This attitude, along with the sheer luxury of life in the U.S. and the obvious relativism and decadence of so much of its complex culture, accounts for much of the resentment that is directed at the U.S. by others in the world (along with greed, self-absorption and/or self-serving guilt, entitlement, lack of interest in international politics, "psychic numbing," and the spreading of consumer culture to "help" others…).

The pain of developmental challenge arises from the fact that these attitudes were so largely unconscious in the past. Coming to consciousness is always painful. The situation of the U.S. at this point in history is analogous to that of an individual coming to the developmental threshold whereby we become aware of ego self and begin to take responsibility for our limitations and the injuries we have inflicted on others. Indeed, this developmental threshold seems to be at the center of history for both individuals and nations/cultures in this pivotal time. It entails the movement to a maturity in which we can calmly stand apart from what we have been before, overriding the age-old defensiveness that causes us to insist on our own perfection and place all blame on the other.

The challenge is huge: because this defensiveness has driven so much of human history, and because the space of "calm standing" seems so unfamiliar and insecure. Yet it seems fair to say that we must meet this challenge if we are to have a future of peace and justice.

One essential quality of crossing over into the broader maturity that our time both induces and requires is self-respect: the ability to not only criticize self and past actions, but also to honor and cultivate the best of what we have been struggling to be and become. And in this the U.S. is blessed, and perhaps has a special gift and obligation to the rest of the world. For the positive and opportunity side of the crisis is a wider and more inclusive embodiment of the very ideals that are at the root of what has been called "the American experiment": a republic of humankind, a unity in diversity, a pluralistic society/world. America needs to confess failures both at home and abroad in the implementation of these ideals. But it also needs to honor and enjoy the relative success that has been achieved.

The opportunity side of the present is that the U.S. itself could now stand with other nations/cultures in the same relational ideal we have tried to foster at home. Unity with other nations/cultures, *against* the commonly shared threat of terrorism/fanaticism from both without and within could also be an occasion in which we stand *for* what we have stood for from the beginning. It may even be possible for the U.S. to advocate the best of its own tradition while affirming that other nations/cultures can also live the same occasion and offer their best to the emerging reality of humankind. This seems crucial: that offering our best requires openness to the best of what others have to offer, and a mutual commitment to continued growth. For example, we have much to learn from Chinese culture about cultivation of the democratic personality that is necessary to sustaining democratic community.[168]

And this openness, which is paradoxically necessary to the health of our own advocacy, could help the U.S. domestically as well—toward a more full embodiment of our magnificent ideals of democracy and world citizenship.

CHAPTER SEVEN

DIALOGUE QUESTIONS

1. In the immediacy of my actual life, what is the service dimension and how could it be refined and cultivated?

2. Where in the world do I see (or choose to believe in) creativity, progress, hope? How is my own service connected to this sense of larger vitality?

3. What is my philosophical or religious reason for valuing service (...or not)?

ENDNOTES

Chapter One

1. Plato, *Theaeteus* 155d, in *The Collected Dialogues of Plato,* ed. Edith Hamilton and Huntington Cairns, Bollingen Series, no. 71 (New York: Pantheon Books, 1985), p. 860.
2. Huston Smith, "Western Philosophy as a Great Religion," in *Huston Smith: Essays on World Religion,* ed. M. Darrol Bryant (New York: Paragon House, 1992), p. 217.
3. Jacob Needleman, *Time and the Soul* (New York: Doubleday, 1998), p. 127.
4. Plato, *Socrates' Defense (Apology)* 38a, in *The Collected Dialogues of Plato,* p. 23.
5. Ibid., 23b, p. 9.
6. Huston Smith, *Forgotten Truth: The Common Vision of the World's Religions* (San Francisco: HarperSanFrancisco, 1976). See also Huston Smith, "Is there a Perennial Philosophy?" *Journal of the American Academy of Religion,* Vol. 55, no. 3 (fall 1987), pp. 553–566.
7. Plato, *Meno* 80a, in *The Collected Dialogues of Plato*, p 363.
8. See also my previous work, especially *Rediscovering the West: An Inquiry into Nothingness and Relatedness* (Albany, NY: SUNY Press, 1994), and *Leaving and Returning: On America's Contribution to a World Ethic* (Lewisburg, PA: Bucknell University Press, 1989).
9. Vaclav Havel, *Living in Truth* (Boston: Faber and Faber, 1989), pp. 44-57.
10. Hannah Arendt, "Karl Jaspers: Citizen of the World?" in *Men in Dark Times* (New York: Harcourt, Brace & World, 1955), pp. 81–94.
11. William James, *Essays in Radical Empiricism and a Pluralistic Universe* (New York: Dutton, 1971), p. 265.
12. On philosophy as practice, see: Pierre Hadot, *Philosophy as a Way of Life: Spiritual Exercises from Socrates to Foucault* (Cambridge, MA: Blackwell, 1995); Mark Moes, *Plato's Dialogue Form and the Care of the Soul* (New York: Peter Lang, 2000); Jacob Needleman, *The Heart of Philosophy: Toward a New Consciousness—Ideas that Challenge, Enlighten and Reshape Our Lives and Our World* (New York: Bantam, 1984); and Martha Nussbaum, *The Therapy of Desire: Theory and Practice in Hellenistic Ethics* (Princeton: Princeton University Press, 1994).
13. Alfred North Whitehead, *Process and Reality* (New York: Free Press) p. 10.

14. James, *Essays,* p. 150.
15. Rainer Maria Rilke, *Letters to a Young Poet* (New York: Vintage Books, 1986), p. 34.
16. Elizabeth Kamarck Minnich, *Transforming Knowledge* (Philadelphia: Temple University Press, 1990), p. 11. On the relationship between conversation and writing, see also David Tracy, *Plurality and Ambiguity: Hermeneutics, Religion, Hope* (San Francisco: Harper & Row, 1987).
17. Plato, *Phaedo 63b–69*, in *The Collected Dialogues of Plato,* pp. 45–52.
18. For a useful presentation of this spectrum, see James, *Essays,* "The Types of Philosophic Thinking," pp. 123–141.
19. For an overview of the contemporary situation in philosophy, including substantiation of my claim about the waning of the analytical dominance, see: Kenneth Baynes, James Bohman, Thomas McCarthy, eds., *After Philosophy: End or Transformation?* (Cambridge, MA: MIT Press, 1996); Richard J. Bernstein, *Philosophical Profiles: Essays in a Pragmatic Mode* (Philadelphia: University of Pennsylvania Press, 1986), *Post-Analytical Philosophy,* ed. John Rajchman, Cornell West (New York: Columbia University Press, 1985); Stephen Toulmin, *Return to Reason* (Cambridge, MA: Harvard University Press, 2001); and Bruce Wilshire, *The Moral Collapse of the University: Professionalization, Purity, and Alienation* (Albany, NY: SUNY Press, 1990).

Chapter Two

20. Plato, *Phaedo* 77e, in *The Collected Dialogues of Plato,* p. 61.
21. Nel Noddings, *Caring: A Feminine Approach to Ethics and Moral Education* (Berkeley: University of California Press, 1984), p. 49.
22. William James, *Talks to Teachers on Psychology: and to Students on Some of Life's Ideals,* Intro. Paul Woodring (New York: W. W. Norton, 1958), p. 39.
23. I provide a more full account of "leaving" in *Leaving and Returning,* especially in "Modern History as Forgetting—and Remembering (a Reflection on the Sixties)," pp. 99–117.
24. Plato, *Socrates' Defense (Apology),* in *The Collected Dialogues of Plato,* pp. 3–26.
25. Smith, "Western Philosophy as a Great Religion," pp. 205–223.
26. Plato, *Phaedo,*in *The Collected Dialogues of Plato,* pp. 40–98.
27. Noddings, *Caring,* pp. 104–131.
28. James, "The Types of Philosophic Thinking," in *Essays,* p. 128.
29. Martin Luther King Jr., "The World House," in *Where Do We Go from Here: Chaos or Community?* (Boston: Beacon Press, 1967).
30. Masao Abe, "Zen Is Not a Philosophy, But…," in *Zen and Western Thought* (Honolulu: University of Hawaii Press, 1985), pp. 3-24.
31. Karl Jaspers, "The Maintenance of Selfhood in the Contemporary Situation," in *Man in the Modern Age,* Eden and Cedar Paul, trs. (Garden City, NY: Anchor Books, 1957), pp. 193–217.

Chapter Three

32. William James, "The Types of Philosophic Thinking," in *Essays,* p. 126.
33. Plato, *Phaedo* 114d, in *The Collected Dialogues of Plato,* pp. 94-95.
34. Robert M. Pirsig, *Zen and the Art of Motorcycle Maintenance* (New York: William Morrow, 1974), p. 242. Pirsig's novel very effectively engages philosophy through literature. I note another novel that can be recommended in the same genre: Jostein Gaarder, *Sophie's World* (New York: Berkle, 1996).
35. Lao Tzu, *Tao Te Ching,* trans. Gia-Fu Feng and Jane English, intro and notes Jacob Needleman (New York: Vintage Books, 1989), p. 3.
36. Karl Jaspers, *The Origin and Goal of History* (New Haven: Yale University Press, 1953). For a helpful discussion of the Historical Period and Jaspers' discoveries, see Robert N. Bellah, "Religious Evolution," in *Beyond Belief: Essays on Religion in a Post-Traditional World* (New York: Harper and Row, 1970), pp. 20–50, and Arendt, "Karl Jaspers: Citizen of the World?" pp. 81–94. Both of these essays are included in my anthology, *Living Beyond Crisis: Essays on Discovery and Being in the World* (New York: Pilgrim Press, 1980).
37. King, "The World House," p. 171.
38. Bellah, "Religious Evolution," p. 40.
39. Hans-George Gadamer, *Truth and Method* (New York: Crossroad, 1988), pp. 323, 324.
40. Hannah Arendt, *The Origins of Totalitarianism* (Cleveland: Meridian Books, 1958), p. 413.
41. Tracy, *Plurality and Ambiguity,* pp. 93–94.
42. William James, "What Pragmatism Means," in *The Writings of William James: A Comprehensive Edition,* ed. John J. McDermott (Chicago: University of Chicago Press, 1977), pp. 389–390. For my selection and presentation of William James, see Stephen Rowe, *The Vision of James* (London: Vega, 2001).
43. James, "The Will to Believe," in *The Writings of William James,* pp. 717–35, especially p. 731.
44. On the relationship between pragmatism and feminism, see Charlene Haddock Seigfried, *Pragmatism and Feminism: Reweaving the Social Fabric* (Chicago: University of Chicago Press, 1996).
45. Noddings, *Caring,* p. 35.
46. Minnich, *Transforming Knowledge,* p. 184.
47. See, for example, Plato, *Symposium* 220c–d, in *The Collected Dialogues of Plato,* p. 571.
48. Abe, *Zen and Western Thought,* pp. 274–275.
49. Bellah, "Religious Evolution," p. 42.
50. James, *Essays,* p. 272.
51. Plato, *Socrates' Defense (Apology) 20d, 21d,* in *The Collected Dialogues of Plato,* pp. 7, 8.

Chapter Four

52. Plato, *Socrates' Defense (Apology)* 29d–e, 30a–b, in *The Collected Dialogues of Plato*, p. 16.
53. King, "The World House," p. 171.
54. Minnich, *Transforming Knowledge*, pp. 29–30.
55. James, *Essays*, p. 260.
56. Ibid., p. 150.
57. I detail this understanding of James in "Revitalizing Practice: A Conversational Encounter with William James," in Rowe, *The Vision of James*, pp. 15–48.
58. Ayn Rand, *Atlas Shrugged* (New York: Plume, 1999). See also Ayn Rand, *The Virtue of Selfishness* (New York: New American Library, 1964).
59. Wilshire, *The Moral Collapse of the University*, p. 12
60. T. S. Eliot, "Choruses from 'The Rock.'" In *The Complete Poems and Plays: 1909-1950* (New York: Harcourt Brace, 1952), p. 96.
61. See William Barrett, *Death of the Soul: From Descartes to the Computer* (Garden City, NY: Anchor Press, 1986).
62. For a brilliant discussion of the Kafka story and its implications, see William Barrett, *The Illusion of Technique* (Garden City, NY: Anchor Books, 1979), p. 68.
63. Richard Stivers, *The Culture of Cynicism: American Morality in Decline* (Cambridge, MA: Blackwell, 1994), p. 112.
64. Havel, "The Power of the Powerless," in *Living in Truth*, p. 115.
65. Hannah Arendt, *Eichmann in Jerusalem: A Report on the Banality of Evil* (New York: Viking Press, 1963), p. 289.
66. Alfred North Whitehead, *Science and the Modern World* (New York: Free Press, 1967), p. 197.
67. Havel, "The Power of the Powerless," p. 54.
68. George Soros, "The Capitalist Threat," in *Atlantic Monthly*, vol. 279, no. 2, February 1997, pp. 45–58.
69. For a helpful discussion of the Psychological Worldview, roughly along the lines of my presentation, see: Stewart Justman, *The Psychological Mystique* (Evanston, IL: Northwestern University Press, 1999); Ellen Herman, *The Romance of Psychology: Political Culture in the Age of Experts* (Berkeley: University of California Press, 1995); and James Hillman and Michael Ventura, *We've Had a Hundred Years of Psychotherapy—and the World's Getting Worse* (San Francisco: Harper SanFrancisco, 1992).
70. Philip Rieff, *The Triumph of the Therapeutic: Uses of Faith After Freud* (New York: Harper Torchbooks, 1966), p. 13.
71. Hannah Arendt, The Origins of Totalitarianism (Cleveland: Meridian Books, 1958), p. 364.
72. Plato, *Meno* 95–99a, in *The Collected Dialogues of Plato*, pp. 379–382.
73. Doris Lessing, *The Four-Gated City* (New York: Bantam Books, 1970), p. 223.

74. Friedrich Nietzsche, *The Genealogy of Morals*, in *The Birth of Tragedy and The Genealogy of Morals*, trans. Francis Golffing (Garden City, NY: Doubleday Anchor, 1956), p. 299.
75. Ira Progoff, *The Death and Rebirth of Psychology* (New York: McGraw-Hill, 1973), p. 15.
76. See *The Cambridge Dictionary of Philosophy*, ed., Robert Audi (New York: Cambridge University Press, 1995), pp. 752-753.

Chapter Five

77. Plato, *Socrates' Defense (Apology)* 40a, see also 31d, in *The Collected Dialogues of Plato*, p. 24.
78. Masao Abe, "Education in Zen," in *The Eastern Buddhist*, n.s. IX, no. 2 (October 1976), p. 237.
79. Vaclav Havel, "The Power of the Powerless," in *Living the Truth*, pp. 115-122.
80. King, "The World House," p. 186.
81. Jaspers, "The Maintenance of Selfhood in the Contemporary Situation," p. 214.
82. Havel, "The Power of the Powerless," p. 54.
83. Carol Gilligan, *In a Different Voice: Psychological Theory and Women's Development* (Cambridge, MA: Harvard University Press, 1982), pp. 173–174.
84. Elizabeth Kubler-Ross, *On Death and Dying* (New York: Touchstone, 1997).
85. Gilligan, *In a Different Voice*, chapter 6, "Visions of Maturity," pp. 151–174.
86. Dietrich Bonhoeffer, *Letters and Papers from Prison*, ed. Eberhard Bethge (New York: Macmillan, 1976), p. 381.
87. Plato, *Phaedo* 77e, in *The Collected Dialogues of Plato*, p. 61.
88. Robert N. Bellah, "Religious Evolution," p. 42.
89. Nietzsche, *The Genealogy of Morals*, p. 299.
90. Keiji Nishitani, *Religion and Nothingness*, trans. and intro, Jan Van Bragt (Berkeley: University of California Press, 1982), p. 151.
91. Plato, *Republic* 532b, in *The Collected Dialogues of Plato*, p. 764.
92. Eliot, "Choruses from 'The Rock'," in *The Complete Poems*, p. 96.
93. Jaspers, "The Maintenance of Selfhood" in *Man in the Modern Age*, p. 193.
94. For initial sources on meditation practice, see: Thich Nhat Hanh, *The Miracle of Mindfulness: A Manual on Meditation* (Boston: Beacon, 1977), William Johnston, *Christian Zen: A Way of Meditation* (San Francisco: Harper & Row, 1971), Jack Kornfield, *A Path with Heart: A Guide Through the Perils and Promises of Spiritual Life* (New York: Bantam, 1993), and John Kabat-Zinn, *Wherever You Go There You Are: Mindfulness Meditation in Everyday Life* (New York: Hyperion, 1994).
95. See Herbert Benson with Marg Stark, *Timeless Healing: The Power and Biology of Belief* (New York: Simon & Schuster, 1997).
96. Paul Tillich, *Systematic Theology*, vol. 3 (Harper & Row and University of Chicago Press, 1967), p. 231.

97. Henry Nelson Wieman, *The Source of Human Good* (Carbondale, IL: Southern Illinois University Press, 1946), p. 58.
98. Hannah Arendt, *The Human Condition* (Chicago: University of Chicago Press, 1958), pp. 177–78.
99. See Jaspers, *The Origin and Goal of History;* Bellah, "Religious Evolution"; Arendt, "Karl Jaspers: Citizen of the World?"
100. King, "The World House," p. 178.
101. Tu Weiming, "Epilogue: Human Rights as a Confucian Moral Discourse," in Wm. Theodore de Bary and Tu Weiming, eds., *Confucianism and Human Rights* (New York: Columbia, 1985), p. 299.
102. For a powerful articulation of the greatness of the American tradition of voluntary associations, see James Luther Adams, *Voluntary Associations: Socio-Cultural Analysis and Theological Interpretation,* ed. J. Ronald Engel (Chicago: Exploration Press, 1986). For my presentation and critique of Adams, see "Toward a Postliberal Liberalism: James Luther Adams and the Need for a Theory of Relational Meaning," in *American Journal of Theology & Philosophy,* vol. 17, no. 1 (January 1996), pp. 51–70. In my work I present the greatness of this same tradition in terms of "the creating form of association." See *Leaving and Returning,* pp. 99–105, 131–35.
103. On service learning in philosophy, see C. David Lisman and Irene E. Harvey, eds., *Beyond the Tower: Concepts and Models for Service-Learning in Philosophy* (Washington, DC: American Association for Higher Education, 2000). I also refer the interested reader to the award-winning service learning program in my home department at Grand Valley State University: www.gvsu.edu/philosophy
104. Etty Hillesum, *An Interrupted Life: The Diaries of Etty Hillesum 1941–43,* trans. Arno Pomerans (New York: Washington Square Press, 1981), pp. 186–187.
105. William James, in McDermott, ed. *The Writings of William James, p.* 7.

Chapter Six

106. Jaspers, "The Maintenance of Selfhood in the Contemporary Situation," p. 198.
107. Lao Tzu, *Tao Te Ching,* p. 73.
108. King, "The World House," p. 171.
109. Jaspers, "The Maintenance of Selfhood in the Contemporary Situation."
110. For insight on the complex relationship between the public and the private, see Hannah Arendt, *The Human Condition,* especially Chapter 2, "The Public and the Private Realm," pp. 22–78, and John K. Roth, *Private Needs, Public Selves: Talk about Religion in America* (Chicago: University of Illinois Press, 1997).
111. David Lubbers, Stephen Rowe, *Abiding: Landscape of the Soul* (Grand Rapids, MI: Eerdmans, 1998)
112. Peimin Ni, Stephen Rowe, *Wandering: Brush and Pen in Philosophical Reflection.* (Shanghai: Donfang Publishers; Chicago: Art Media Resources, 2002).

113. Sissela Bok, *Lying: Moral Choice in Public and Private Life* (New York: Vintage, 1979), especially Chapter 1, "Is the Whole Truth Attainable?," pp. 3–17.
114. For a helpful discussion of proteanness and its implications, see Robert Jay Lifton, *History and Human Survival* (New York: Vintage, 1971).
115. Laura Duhan Kaplan, *Family Pictures: A Philosopher Explores the Familiar* (Chicago: Open Court, 1998).
116. King, "The World House," p. 180.
117. Aristotle, *Nicomachean Ethics,* in Richard McKeon, ed., *The Basic Works of Aristotle* (New York: Random House, 1966), p. 956.
118. Wieman, *The Source of Human Good,* p. 22.
115. Anne Morrow Lindbergh, *Gift from the Sea* (New York: Pantheon, 1955), pp. 98–99, 124–125.
119. Riane Eisler, *The Chalice and the Blade* (San Francisco: HarperSanFrancisco, 1988).
120. Richard Tarnas, *The Passion of the Western Mind* (New York: Ballantine, 1991), pp. 141, 145.
121. Tarnas, *Passion of the Western Mind,* p. 444.
123. See Hannah Arendt, *On Revolution* (New York: Viking Press, 1963).
124. Robin Morgan, *Going Too Far: The Personal Chronicle of a Feminist* (New York: Vintage, 1978), p. 3.
125. Karl Jaspers, "Situation in General," in *Man in the Modern Age,* p. 26.
126. Martin Buber, *I and Thou,* trans. with prologue, Walter Kaufman (New York: Charles Scribner's Sons, 1970).
127. Rowe, *Leaving and Returning,* pp. 102–5.
128. Huston Smith, *Why Religion Matters: The Fate of the Human Spirit in the Age of Disbelief* (San Francisco: HarperSanFrancisco, 2001), p. xiii.
129. Adrienne Rich, "Women and Honor: Some Notes on Lying," in Stephen Rowe, ed., *Living Beyond Crisis: Essays on Discovery and Being in the World* (New York: Pilgrim, 1980), p. 71.
130. Hannah Arendt, "Karl Jaspers: Citizen of the World," p. 85.
131. Jaspers, "Situation in General," p. 26.
132. Soros, "The Capitalist Threat."
133. Paul Valéry, cited in Barrett, *The Illusion of Technique,* p. 332.
134. Rich, "Women and Honor," p. 71.
135. See Joan Didion, "On Self-Respect," in *Slouching Towards Bethlehem* (New York: Touchstone, 1979), pp. 142–148.
136. Nel Noddings, *Caring,* p. 115.
137. For a discussion of forgivenness, see *Utne Reader,* no. 92 (March–April 1999), pp. 44–59.
138. Stanley Rosen, *The Ancients and the Moderns: Rethinking Modernity* (New Haven: Yale University Press, 1989), p. 36.
139. Peter D. Hershock, *Reinventing the Wheel: A Buddhist Response to the Informa-*

tion Age (Albany, NY: SUNY Press, 2001), p. 287. This book, especially the last chapter."So What?," is a brilliant presentation of Buddhist practice as remedy for "the colonialization of consciousness" that is already well developed in something like what I call "Machinism."

140. Ralph Harper, *On Presence: Variations and Reflections* (Philadelphia: Trinity Press International, 1991), p. 70.
141. See Robert E. Cushman, *Therapeia: Plato's Conception of Philosophy* (Westport, CN: Grenwood Press, 1958).
142. Richard Stivers, *The Culture of Cynicism.*
143. Ni and Rowe, *Wandering.*
144. Hillesum, *An Interrupted Life,* p. 181.
145. Confucius, *Analects*, 15/29. For discussion of this point and Confucianism generally, see Peimin Ni, *On Confucius* (Belmont, CA: Wadsworth, 2001), especially p. 94.
146. Madeleine L'Engle, *A Wrinkle in Time* (New York: Farrar, Straus and Giroux, 1962).
147. For presentation of scientific evidence on qigong practice, see Lu Zuyin, *Scientific Qigong Exploration: The Wonders and Mysteries of Qi* (Malvern, PA: Amber Leaf Press, 1997), and Hao Wang, Jo Ann Wozniak, Stevenson Wu, *Yan Xin Qicong and the Contemporary Sciences* (Urbana-Champaign, IL: International Yan Xin Qicong Association, 1991).
148. Benson, *Timeless Healing.*

Chapter 7

149. Elizabeth Minnich, *Transforming Knowledge,* p. 179.
150. Tu Weiming, "Implications of the Rise of 'Confucian' East Asia, in *Daedalus: Journal of the American Academy of Arts and Sciences,* vol. 129, no.1 (winter 2000), p. 196.
151. On the necessity of including religious traditions in the discussion about global governance and overcoming the modern division between religion and politics, see Richard Falk, *Religion and Humane Global Governance* (New York: Palgrave, 2001).
152. On the meaning and dimensions of dialogue, see John B. Cobb Jr., *Beyond Dialogue: Toward a Mutual Transformation of Christianity and Buddhism* (Philadelphia: Fortress Press, 1982).
153. See Huston Smith, *Beyond the Post-Modern Mind* (New York: Crossroad, 1982).
154. My thinking on human development has been informed by: James W. Fowler, *Stages of Faith: The Psychology of Human Development and the Quest for Meaning* (San Francisco: Harper & Row, 1981); Carol Gilligan, *In a Different Voice;* Lawrence Kohlberg, *The Philosophy of Moral Development: Moral Stages and the Idea of*

Justice (San Francisco: Harper & Row1981); William Perry, *Forms of Intellectual and Moral Development in the College Years* (New York: Holt, Rinehart and Winston: 1968); and Gail Sheehy, *Passages: Predictable Crises of Adult Life* (New York: Dutton, 1974).

155. This theme is developed more fully in my *Rediscovering the West.*
156. For a Chinese perspective on the Modern and modernization, see Tong Shijun, *The Dialectics of Modernization: Habermas and the Chinese Discourse of Modernization* (Sidney: Wild Peony, 2000).
157. Richard Rorty, *Contingency, Irony, and Solidarity* (Cambridge: Cambridge University Press, 1989), p. 53.
158. Tu Weiming in Ni and Rowe, *Wandering*. See William James on the need for reform in philosophy in order "to apprehend reality's thickness," in *Essays,* p. 240.
159. Plato, *Socrates' Defense (*Apology) 38a, in *The Collected Dialogues of Plato,* p. 23.
160. Ibid. 30b–31c, pp. 16–17.
161. Plato, *Symposium* 220c–d, in *The Collected Dialogues of Plato,* p. 571; Plato, *Socrates' Defense* (Apology) 30d, 40a, in *The Collected Dialogues of Plato,* pp. 17, 24.
162. Plato, *Socrates' Defense (Apology)* 40a, p. 24.
163. Smith, "Western Philosophy as a Great Religion."
164. Smith, *Forgotten Truth.*
165. Tu Weiming, "Implications of the Rise of 'Confucian' East Asia."
166. Hannah Arendt, *The Human Condition,* p. 176.
167. Plato, *Letters VII 241c–d,* in *The Collected Dialogues of Plato,* p. 1589.
168. On Chinese cultivation of the person, see Peimin Ni, "*Xue—Learning to be Human,*" in *On Confucius,* pp. 86–96. Out of dialogue with Chinese philosophy generally, I am led to the thesis that the West has had the *form* of democracy, but has lacked the personal development necessary in order to sustain this ideal intellectually grasped, while the East has had the *substance* of individual development but has lacked the democratic ideal as a political aspiration. This thesis, of course, is quite discussable. In its support here I will simply say that, as a Westerner who has often been frustrated in efforts to support democratic social change, I have often thought of Mill's remark to the effect that democracy only works among individuals who are "in the maturity of their faculties." See John Stuart Mill "On Liberty," in *Utilitarianism*, ed., Mary Warnock (New York: New American Library, 1974), p. 135.

BIBLIOGRAPHY

Abe, Masao. "Education in Zen" in *The Eastern Buddhist,* n.s. IX, no. 2 (October 1976).

———. *Zen and Western Thought* (Honolulu: University of Hawaii Press, 1985).

Adams, James Luther. *Voluntary Associations: Socio-Cultural Analysis and Theological Interpretation.* Ed. Engel J. Ronald (Chicago: Exloration Press, 1986).

Arendt, Hannah. *Eichmann in Jerusalem: A Report on the Banality of Evil* (New York: Viking Press, 1963).

———. "Karl Jaspers: Citizen of the World?" in *Men in Dark Times* (New York: Harcourt, Brace & World, 1955).

———. *On Revolution* (New York: Viking Press, 1963).

———. *The Human Condition* (Chicago: University of Chicago Press, 1958).

———. *The Origins of Totalitarianism* (Cleveland: Meridian Books, 1958).

Aristotle. *Nicomachean Ethics,* in *The Basic Works of Aristotle,* ed. Richard McKeon, (New York: Random House, 1996).

Audi, Robert. ed., *The Cambridge Dictionary of Philosophy* (New York: Cambridge University Press, 1995).

Barrett, William. *Death of the Soul: From Descartes to the Computer* (Garden City, NY: Anchor Press, 1979).

———. *The Illusion of Technique* (Garden City, NY: Anchor Press, 1986).

Baynes, Kenneth; James Bohman; and Thomas McCarthy, eds. *After Philosophy: End or Transformation?* (Cambridge, MA: MIT Press, 1996).

Bellah, Robert N. *Beyond Belief: Essays on Religion in a Post-Traditional World* (New York: Harper and Row, 1970).

Benson, Herbert. *Timeless Healing: The Power and Biology of Belief* (New York: Simon & Schuster, 1997).

Bernstein, Richard J. *Philosophical Profiles: Essays in a Pragmatic Mode* (Philadelphia: University of Pennsylvania Press, 1986).

———. *Post-Analytical Philosophy,* eds. John Rajchman, Cornell West (New York: Columbia University Press, 1985).

Bok, Sissela. *Lying: Moral Choice in Public and Private Life* (New York: Vintage, 1979).

Bonhoeffer, Dietrich. *Letters and Papers from Prison.* Ed. Eberhard Bethge (New York: Macmillan, 1976).

Buber, Martin. *I and Thou,* trans. with prologue, Walter Kaufman (New York: Charles Scribner's Sons, 1970).

Cobb, John B. Jr. *Beyond Dialogue: Toward a Mutual Transformation of Christianity and Buddhism* (Philadelphia: Fortress Press, 1982).

Cushman, Robert E. *Therapeia: Plato's Conception of Philosophy* (Westport, CT: Greenwood Press, 1958).

Didion, Joan. "On Self-Respect," in *Slouching Towards Bethlehem* (New York: Touchstone, 1979).

Eisler, Riane. The Chalice and the Blade (San Francisco: HarperSanFrancisco, 1988).

Eliot, T. S. "Choruses from 'The Rock'," in *The Complete Poems and Plays, 1909-1950* (New York: Harcourt Brace, 1952).

Falk, Richard. *Religion and Human Global Governance* (New York: Palgrave, 2001).

Fowler, James W. *Stages of Faith: The Psychology of Human Development and the Quest for Meaning* (San Francisco: Harper & Row, 1981).

Gaarder, Jostein. *Sophie's World* (New York: Berkle, 1996).

Gadamer, Hans-Georg. *Truth and Method* (New York: Crossroad, 1988).

Gilligan, Carol. *In a Different Voice: Psychological Theory and Women's Development* (Cambridge, MA: Harvard University Press, 1982).

Hadot, Pierre. *Philosophy as a Way of Life: Spiritual Exercises from Socrates to Foucault* (Cambridge, MA: Blackwell, 1995).

Hanh, Thich Nhat. *The Miracle of Mindfulness: A Manual on Meditation* (Boston: Beacon, 1977).

Harper, Ralph. *On Presence: Variations and Reflections* (Philadelphia: Trinity Press International, 1991).

Harvey, Irene E. and C. David Lisman, eds. *Beyond the Tower: Concepts and Models for Service-Learning in Philosophy* (Washington, DC: American Association for Higher Education, 2000).

Havel, Vaclav. *Living in Truth* (Boston: Faber and Faber, 1989).

Herman, Ellen. *The Romance of Psychology: Political Culture in the Age of Experts* (Berkeley: University of California Press, 1995).

Hershock, Peter D. *Reinventing the Wheel: A Buddhist Response to the Information Age* (Albany, New York: Suny Press, 2001).

Hillesum, Etty. *An Interrupted Life: The Diaries of Etty Hillesum 1941-43.* Trans. Arno Pomerans (New York: Washington Square Press, 1981).

Hillman, James and Michael Ventura. *We've had a Hundred Years of Psychoterapy—and the World's Getting Worse* (San Francisco: HarperSanFrancisco, 1992).

James, William. *Essays in Radical Empiricism and a Pluralistic Universe* (New York: Dutton, 1971).
———. Talks to Teachers on Psychology: and to Students on some of Life's Ideals." Introduction by Woodring Paul (New York: W.W. Norton, 1958).
———. *The Writings of William James: A Comprehensive Edition.* Ed. McDermott John J. (Chicago: University of Chicago Press, 1977).
Jaspers, Karl. "The Maintenance of Selfhood in the Contemporary Situation" in *Man in the Modern Age.* Trans. Eden and Cedar Paul (Garden City, NY: Anchor Books,1957).
———. *The Origin and Goal of History* (New Haven: Yale University Press, 1953).
Johnston, William. *Christian Zen: A Way of Meditation* (San Francisco: Harper & Row, 1971).
Justman, Stewart. *The Psychological Mystique* (Evanston, IL: Northwestern University Press, 1999).
Kabat-Zinn, John. *Wherever You Go There You Are: Mindfulness Meditation in Everyday Life* (New York: Hyperion, 1994).
Kaplan, Laura Duhan. *Family Pictures: A Philosopher Explores the Familiar* (Chicago: Open Court, 1998).
King, Martin Luther Jr. *Where Do We Go From Here: Chaos or Community?* (Boston: Beacon Press, 1967).
Kohlberg, Lawrence. *The Philosophy of Moral Development: Moral Stages and the Idea of Justice* (San Francisco: Harper & Row, 1981).
Kornfield, Jack. *A Path with Heart: A Guide Through the Perils and Promises of Spiritual Life* (New York: Bantam, 1993).
Kubler-Ross, Elizabeth. *On Death and Dying* (New York: Touchstone, 1997).
Lao-Tzu. *Tao Te Ching.* Trans. Jane English and Gia-Fu Feng, intro and notes Jacob Needleman (New York: Vintage Books, 1989).
L'Engle, Madeleine. *A Wrinkle in Time* (New York: Farrar, Straus and Giroux, 1962).
Lessing, Doris. *The Four-Gated City* (New York: Bantam Books, 1970).
Lifton, Robert Jay. *History and Human Survival* (New York: Vintage, 1971).
Lindbergh, Anne Morrow. *Gift from the Sea* (New York: Pantheon, 1955).
Lubbers, David and Stephen Rowe. *Abiding: Landscape of the Soul* (Grand Rapids, MI: Eerdmans, 1998).
Mill, John Stuart. "On Liberty", in *Utilitarianism.* Mary Warnock, ed. (New York: New American Library, 1974).
Minnich, Elizabeth Kamarck. *Transforming Knowledge* (Philadelphia: Temple University Press, 1990).
Moes, Mark. *Plato's Dialogue Form and the Care of the Soul* (New York: Peter Lang, 2000).

Morgan, Robin. *Going Too Far: The Personal Chronicle of a Feminist* (New York: Vintage, 1978).
Needleman, Jacob. *Time and the Soul* (New York: Doubleday, 1998).
———. *American Soul* (New York: Putnam Publishing Group, 2002).
Ni, Peimin. *Confucius* (Belmont, CA: Wadsworth, 2001).
———. and Stephen Rowe. *Wandering: Brush and Pen in Philosophical Reflection* (Shanghai: Dongfang Publishers; Chicago: Art Media Resources, 2002).
Nietzsche, *The Genealogy of Morals,* in *The Birth of Tragedy and The Genealogy of Morals.* Trans. Francis Golffing (Garden City, NY: Doubleday Anchor, 1956).
Nishitani, Keiji. *Religion and Nothingness.* Trans. and intro. Jan Van Bragt (Berkeley: University of California Press, 1982).
Noddings, Nel. *Caring: A Feminine Approach to Ethics and Moral Education* (Berkeley: University of California Press, 1984).
Nussbaum, Martha. *The Therapy of Desire: Theory and Practice in Hellenistic Ethics* (Princeton: Princeton University Press, 1994).
Perry, William. *Forms of Intellectual and Moral Develpoment in the College Years* (New York: Holt, Rinehart and Winston, 1968).
Pirsig, Robert M. *Zen and the Art of Motorcycle Maintenance* (New York: William Morrow, 1974).
Plato. *The Collected Dialogues of Plato* Ed. Hutington Cairns and Edith Hamilton, Bollingen Series, no. 71 (New York: Pantheon Books, 1985).
Progoff, Ira. *The Death and Rebirth of Psychology* (New York: McGraw-Hill, 1973).
Rajchman John, Cornell West eds. *Post-Analytical Philosophy* (New York: Columbia University Press, 1985).
Rand, Ayn. *Atlas Shrugged* (New York: Plume, 1999).
———. *The Virtue of Selfishness* (New York: New American Library, 1964).
Rich, Adrienne. "Women and Honor: Some Notes on Lying," in Stephen Rowe, ed. *Living Beyond Crisis: Essays on Discovery and Being in the World* (New York: Pilgrim, 1980).
Rieff, Philip. *The Triumph of the Therapeutic: Uses of Faith After Freud* (New York: Harper Torchbooks, 1966).
Rilke, Rainer Maria. *Letters to a Young Poet* (New York: Vintage Books,1986).
Rorty, Richard. *Contingency, Irony and Solidarity* (Cambridge: Cambridge University Press, 1989).
Rosen, Stanley. *The Ancients and the Moderns: Rethinking Modernity* (New Haven: Yale University Press, 1989).
Roth, John K. *Private Needs, Public Selves: Talk About Religion in America* (Chicago: University of Illinois Press, 1997).
Rowe, Stephen. *Leaving and Returning: On America's Contribution to a World*

Ethic (Lewisburg, PA: Bucknell University Press, 1989).
———. *Living Beyond Crisis: Essays on Discovery and Being in the World* (New York: Pilgrim Press, 1980).
———. *Rediscovering the West: An Inquiry into Nothingness and Relatedness* (Albany, NY: SUNY Press, 1994).
———. *The Vision of James* (London: Vega, 2001).
———. "Toward a Postliberal Liberalism: James Luther Adams and the Need for a Theory of Relational Meaning," in *American Journal of Theology & Philosophy,* vol. 17 no. 1 (January 1996).
Seigfried, Charlene Haddock. *Pragmatism and Feminism: Reweaving the Social Fabric* (Chicago: University Press, 1996).
Sheehy, Gail. *Passages: Predictable Crisis of Adult Life* (New York: Dutton, 1974).
Smith, Huston. *Beyond the Post-Modern Mind* (New York: Crossroad, 1982).
———. *Forgotten Truth: The Common Vision of the World's Religions* (San Francisco: HarperSanFransisco, 1976).
———. "Is there a Perennial Philosophy?" *Journal of the American Academy of Religion,* vol. 55, no.3 (fall 1987).
———. "Western Philosophy as a Great Religion", in Huston Smith: *Essays on World Religion.* Ed. M. Darrol Bryant (New York : Paragon House, 1992).
———. *Why Religion Matters: The Fate of the Human Spirit in the Age of Disbelief* (San Francisco: HarperSanFrancisco, 2001).
Soros, George. "The Capitalism Threat," in *Atlantic Monthly* vol. 279, no. 2, Feb. 1997.
Stivers, Richard. *The Culture of Cynicism: American Morality in Decline* (Cambridge, MA: Blackwell, 1994).
Tarnas, Richard. *The Passion of the Western Mind* (New York: Ballantine, 1991).
Tillich, Paul. *Systematic Theology,* vol. 3 (Harper and Row and University of Chicago Press, 1967).
Tong Shijun, *The Dialectics of Modernization: Habermas and the Chinese Discourse of Modernization* (Sidney: Wild Peony, 2002).
Toulmin, Stephen. *Return to Reason,* (Cambridge, MA: Harvard University Press, 2001).
Tracy, David. *Plurality and Ambiguity: Hermeneutics, Religion, Hope* (San Francisco: Harper & Row, 1987).
Tu Weiming. "Epilogue: Human Rights as a Confucian Moral Discourse," in *Confucianism and Human Rights.* Ed. Wm. Theodore de Barye and Tu Weiming (1985).
———. "Implications of the Rise of 'Confucian' East Asia," in *Daedalus: Journal of the American Academy of Arts and Sciences,* Vol. 129, no. 1 (win-

ter 2000).

Utne Reader. No. 92 (March-April 1999).

Wang, Hao, Jo Ann Wozniak, and Stevenson Wu. *Yan Xin Qicong and the Contemporary Sciences* (Urbana-Champaign, IL: International Yan Xin Qicong Association, 1991).

Whitehead, Alfred North. *Process and Reality* (New York: Free Press).

———. *Science and the Modern World* (New York: Free Press, 1967).

Wieman, Henry Nelson. *The Source of Human Good* (Carbondale, IL: Southern Illinois University Press, 1946).

Wilshire, Bruce. *The Moral Collapse of the University: Professionalization, Purity and Alienation* (Albany, NY: SUNY Press, 1990).

Zuyin, Lu. *Scientific Qigong Exploration: The Wonders and Mysteries of Qi* (Malvern, PA: Amber Leaf Press, 1997).

INDEX